H

D0079507

UNIVERSITY OF NEW MEXICO PRESS ALBUQUERQUE

A Cross and A Star

MEMOIRS OF
A JEWISH GIRL
IN CHILE

Marjorie Agosín

TRANSLATED BY
CELESTE KOSTOPULOS-COOPERMAN

© 1995 by the University of New Mexico Press.

All rights reserved.

First edition

Library of Congress Cataloging-in-Publication Data

Agosín, Marjorie

[Sagrada memoria. English]

A cross and a star : memoirs of a Jewish girl in Chile / Marjorie Agosín;

translated by Celeste Kostopulos-Cooperman. — 1st ed.   p.   cm.

Contents: Family alliances—Images of my youth—Osorno—Carmencita
and the kingdom of adobe—The Viennese lady—My husband.

ISBN 0-8263-1573-9 (cloth)

1. Agosín, Marjorie.   2. Jews—Chile—Osorno—Biography.

3. Osorno (Chile)—Biography.   I. Title.

F3285.J4A37   1995

983'.53004924'0092—dc20

[B]   94-3213 CIP

Designed by Linda Mae Tratechaud
Chapter Ornament Illustrations
by Beth Dennis

CONTENTS

INTRODUCTION

*Riches can all be lost, but that happiness in your own
heart can only be veiled, and it will still bring you happiness again, as long as you live. As long as you can look
fearlessly up into the heavens, as long as you know that
you are pure within and that you will still find happiness.*

— Anne Frank, *The Diary of a Young Girl*

In *A Cross and A Star*, Marjorie Agosín recreates a landscape of sounds, colors, and sensorial images that filter
through her poetic vision and depict the personal journey of her mother as a child, adolescent, and young
adult in southern Chile before, during, and after the
Second World War. Significantly the narrative voice
intuitively identifies with Anne Frank before she im-
merses us into the story of her own life with her fears,
anxieties, reflections, and hopes.

Although they lived in worlds apart, in hemispheres and continents separated by the vast expanse of ocean known as the Atlantic, both the young Frida and Anne Frank learned to live with the hatred which surrounded them because of their Jewish identity. As Anne herself writes in her diary, "We Jews mustn't show our feelings, must be brave and strong, must accept all inconveniences and not grumble, must do what is within our power and trust in God. . . . Surely the time will come when we are people again, and not just Jews."[1]

Like Anne, Frida and her brother are constantly aware of their "otherness" in a land where they, together with the poor native children, mostly Indians and mestizos, were marginalized and set apart by a minority that clearly perceived itself as superior and entitled. Throughout her narrative the metaphors of the cross and the star persistently delineate her sense of alienation and exile within a culture that she identifies with but can never fully adopt as her own. Recalling a New Year's Eve in Valparaíso the narrator tells us how she and her brother "always maintained a discrete distance between who they were [the Christian onlookers] and what we were, Jewish children isolated from the grand commotion of the human race." Feeling an affinity to the Christian religion because of the magic of its imagery and mystery of its rituals and wanting to believe that all are equal in the eyes of God and his heavenly chorus of angels, the child narrator, when she is at her most vulnerable, appeals to Christian images hoping that they will shelter her with their sacred charms. However, the sharp and strident memories of little German and English girls spitting at her and calling her a dirty Jew and Christ killer prevent her from trusting and believing in a faith that excluded so many like her from its protective folds.

During the war years, anti-Semitism was particularly high in Chile, especially in southern regions like Osorno where Jews were clearly outnumberd by Germans and other foreigners who had carried their hatreds across the seas in hope chests of evil omens.

Among the first German colonists to arrive in southern Chile were trail blazing individuals who settled in Valdivia, Llanquihue, and Osorno hoping to begin a new life far removed from the disillusionments of their own country's failed democracy. Although there were many nationalists in the second half of the nineteenth century like Dr. Aquinas Ried who envisioned Chile as an asylum for Germans who wanted to preserve their identity in autonomous enclaves that were by and large controlled by their own elected officials, there were others like the pharmacist and philanthropist Karl Anwandter who encouraged his compatriots to assimilate with the native residents in an effort to establish a new life for themselves and their families.

Despite the tensions that developed between the colonizers and Chilean inhabitants and the rising anti-German sentiment that existed at the end of the nineteenth century, the German presence seemed to have invigorated an ailing economy and created much industrial prosperity in places like Valdivia and Osorno. Indeed Osorno at the turn of the century became known as the *Hochburg of Deutschtum* or the Germanic capital of southern Chile. For the Germans who were willing to brave the new world, southern Chile was a haven where they were relatively free to design and administer their own colonies.

Since there were many Germanophiles among Chile's intelligentsia, German immigrants were encouraged to assist in the revitalization of an outmoded pedagogical system as well as in the training and preparation of the country's military officials and the redesign of its armed forces. Bavarian Capuchin missionaries who arrived in the south as cultural messengers were also very successful in the evangelization of Mapuche Indians.

More than any other Latin American country, perhaps with the exception of Argentina, Chile has nurtured most colonization efforts with mainland Germany for well over a century. It is not surprising therefore when we hear about the existence of a place like Dignity Colony, a secluded German enclave about an hour away from Osorno which has existed since the forties. Although travelers are welcomed to visit the tea room where they can feast on perfect apple strudel and other German delicacies, still very little is known about the colony. All attempts of outsiders to gain access to its hidden interiors have failed, even those of the Chilean government, itself. Despite declarations to the contrary, however, it is believed that during the Pinochet years, Dignity Colony was one of the many sites in which victims of the regime were tortured. One has to wonder why "authoritative texts" such as Jean-Pierre Blancpain's *Los alemanes en Chile (1816–1945)* make no mention of this colony as well, nor of the known migrations of Nazi war criminals to Chilean locations.

Chile was an advocate of Hitler's Germany until almost the end of World War II; there was an upsurge of anti-Semitism in Chile during the war years. The narrator recalls the German frenzy that seized her country as well as the racially motivated attacks against herself and her loved ones. The proliferation of German schools, parades, and swastikas were also ample manifestations of the enthusiasm toward the efforts of the Third Reich that gripped Chile at a time when Jews were the primary targets of Hitler's most violent and ruthless racial attacks and were forced to suffer the most extreme indignities before they were annihilated in the death camps.

All references to the war and to the animosities and fears that it engendered push this poetically inspired narrative beyond the borders of traditional autobiography and magnify its universality. *A Cross and A Star* is also a story about foreigners, exiles, and marginalized ethnic and racial groups and their struggle to survive in a land that perceived them as "other." It is a narrative that confronts several issues that assail the human spirit, most particularly that of the grief that surfaces from the depths of human suffering and lingers in the mind and soul when there is no means to recover that which has been lost nor to account fully for its disappearance.

Although *A Cross and A Star* can be compared easily to the narratives of other Latin American Jewish writers who explore issues related to ethnic identity, like the novels of the Peruvian author Isaac Goldemberg and of the Mexicans Rosa Nissan and Margo Glantz, this poetically inspired collage of interrelated prose fragments is unique not only in the field of Chilean literature but also within the larger panorama of contemporary Latin American narrative. It is a book that eludes most standard generic classifications because it is a story that is articulated not by the apparent first-person narrator but through the voice and creative imagination of her poet/writer/child, who is not always able to determine if she tells what she invents or if she invents what she tells. As a chronicler of her mother's life, however, she is bound to stay as close to the truth as is possible so that others will accept the veracity of her story. Tenaciously she admits, "Everything I tell you is true and this is why I write so that it will be even more certain."

It is clear from the very beginning that we are reading a story about a woman who wants to represent herself through the collective fragments of her remembered past. Like an autobiographer she, the mother/daughter narrator, has to rely on memory as her central informing medium. However, as Sidone Smith insightfully observes in *A Poetics of Women's Autobiography*, "memory is ultimately a story about, and thus a discourse on, original experience, so that recovering the past is not a hypostasizing of fixed grounds and absolute origins but, rather, an interpretation of earlier experience that can never be divorced from the filtering of

subsequent experience or articulated outside the structures of language and storytelling."[2] As such, autobio-
graphical writing is a problematic genre because the act
of telling a story is in and of itself a "fictive process." As
Smith reveals, "The autobiographe constantly tells 'a'
story rather than 'the' story, and tells it 'this' way rather
than 'that' way. The reader allows the autobiographer
to create her fiction, knowing that it is, . . . because
every life contains within it multiple discourses on discourses, stories on stories.[3]

As a personal record that is based upon her mother's
recollections of the past, it seems most appropriate to
compare this narrative to a memoir, a very private and
unique form of writing that is capable, in varying de-
grees, of capturing the essence and spirit of the times
about which it is written. Although similar to a diary, it
distinguishes itself by its very desire to be shared with
future generations as well as by its underlying hope to
validate and sustain the intimate story that it contains,
as painful as portions of it may be.

As the memoir unfolds, images of the Holocaust in
all their horror become more powerful and enduring.
Visions of death trains advancing in the darkness, of
smoke-filled skies and blue gas chambers of no return,
of ovens fired by rage, burning forests, barbed wire

camps, abandoned children, and refugees with sad protruding eyes permeate the text and often appear at the
most unexpected of moments. It is almost as if the narrative voice can no longer hold back the flood of memories that are attached to the terrors and anxieties of the
war years and to the tremendous void of the disappeared relatives and loved ones that she never got to
know, like her Aunt Estella from Stanislav and her
Aunt Adela, who was asked to appear at police headquarters one day and was never heard from again.

In this sometimes haunting narrative, the blue vapors of the gas chambers seem to penetrate the multi-
layered memories fusing the destinies of the narrator-
protagonist to those of her departed relatives. For those
familiar with the terror that swept through the southern
cone during the period of the Argentine dirty war (pri-
marily during the decade of the seventies), the image of
Frida's Grandmother Helena approaching the rail stations and carrying photographs of her dead sisters summons up the weekly Thursday afternoon rituals of the
Mothers of the Plaza de Mayo who continue bearing
images of their disappeared loved ones in a *circle of
madness* that seems to have no end. By sanctioning the
"obscure and sinister tactics of making people disappear," the military juntas of the time tragically recov-

ered the Nazi horror and murdered more than thirty thousand people before the world began to take notice.

However, this is not just a story about a woman reminiscing about her own life and about the fate of her relatives and of others who were caught in webs of state-sanctioned terror and in blazing forests of barbed wire camps; it is also an inspiring story about the love and goodwill of an individual whose faith in humanity prevents her from falling into the deepest caverns of despair by allowing her to see beyond the grief and the misery. Interspersed with disconsolate images of sorrow and death are sweet memories of youth that speak to the beauty and generosity of a world flowing with life and hope.

Recollections of colorful figures like her grandmothers Helena and Sonia, her Aunt Lucha, Mrs. Valtiansky, Don Isaac, Mrs. Spirman, and of Olga Tolchinskaya dressed in her long, plush black garments as well as Carmen Carrasco and the many other servants who lived in her household immersing her in their mysterious world of Indian myths and folktales, broaden the cultural landscape of this memoir. It is through her recollected experiences with these individuals that Frida deepens her perceptions of a world that reaches out beyond the rather narrow and geographically isolated territory of her youth, in a country far removed from the threatening spectre of war.

As in *The Diary of Anne Frank*, beautiful images of nature erupt within the narrative flow and remind us that despite the war and its harsh and devastating consequences, there are still spaces, both imaginary and real, where life in all its natural beauty can exist and grow. The narrator-subject's descriptions of autumn and of her almost timeless walks through the wooded paths of the Osorno of her adolescent years, as well as her memories of the seashore and of the star-studded skies and sunflower dawns recall Anne Frank's reflections on the effects of the natural world on the human spirit. Six months before the Gestapo penetrated the Franks' hiding place, Anne's diary entry reads, "I look up at the blue sky and the bare chestnut tree, on whose branches little raindrops shine, appearing like silver, and at the seagulls and the other birds as they glide on the wind. . . . As long as this exists, and it certainly always will, I know that then there will always be comfort for every sorrow, whatever the circumstances may be. And I firmly believe that nature brings solace in all troubles."[4] Similarly Frida, while summarizing the collected fragments of her past, envisions her memory like an immense meadow of bellflowers with trains of refugees approaching and transfigured by the pulse and breath of a new life with songs of peace.

In *A Cross and A Star*, the narrator-protagonist clings to her belief in the basic goodness of humanity and refuses to allow herself to be consumed by the corrosive seeds of animosity and remorse. Even though she, like Anne, has the sensitivity and maturity to realize that dreams and cherished hopes often are shattered by truths which are too horrible to imagine, Frida also prefers to believe that the good will ultimately survive and that "cruelty will end and peace and tranquility will return again."[5]

Although memories fade, transform, and vanish through time, they also maintain our links to the past, giving us the opportunity to reflect upon the experiences that we have had and how they have shaped our perceptions both of ourselves as well as of others. How then do we see ourselves and how are our perceptions of others influenced by our memories and experiences both past and present? Also, how does the venom of hatred, racism, bigotry, and fear affect the lives of the innocent, creating divisions between the self and others that threaten to destroy the foundations of our very humanity by infecting it at the roots? These are questions that are appropriate to address in this late twentieth century where we can witness firsthand the renewed violence and devastation emerging from nationalist movements that condone ethnic cleansing, genocide, and oppression as their primary tools for survival.

Perhaps the loss of hope, the loss of the capacity to dream and to imagine a brighter, more peaceful future for all the peoples of this world is the worst death of all. As we reflect upon the words of the woman-narrator in this poetically articulated memoir, it is hoped that we too will find comfort in her ability to trust and to believe in humanity's unlimited potential to survive the many manifestations of evil that continue to threaten our existence on this earth.

Osorno initially was nothing more than a geographical location on the map. But as I grew familiar with the landscape and the private lives of the people who lived there, it became a vibrant, living community of people who had both a rich and haunting past and a future filled with hope and new beginnings.

It is not possible to experience Osorno and not be touched by the memories of World War II and the atrocities of the Nazi Holocaust. Although the war does not occupy a central position in the narrative, it is always there, living in the mind of the poet-narrator who, because of her Jewishness, is directly affected by the horrors of the war as well as her own sense of alienation within her native yet foreign land, a land starkly different from the European continent of her ancestors.

Osorno quickly became for me more than just a family memoir. Translating it was a way to not only share with others the personal history of a young Jewish girl's life in the southern cone but, more important, a way to make others aware of how the Nazi poison traveled and spread itself to another hemisphere and continent that had itself already suffered from a long history of madness and oppression.

Celeste Kostopulos-Cooperman
Suffolk University
Boston, Massachusetts
June 1994

Notes

1. Anne Frank, *The Diary of a Young Girl* (New York: Simon and Schuster, 1952), p. 186.

2. Sidone Smith, *A Poetics of Women's Autobiography: Marginality and the Fictions of Self-Representation* (Bloomington and Indianapolis: Indiana University Press, 1987), p. 45.

3. Sidone Smith, *A Poetics of Women's Autobiography*, p. 46.

4. Anne Frank, *The Diary of a Young Girl*, p. 143.

5. Ibid. p. 237.

A Cross and A Star

FAMILY ALLIANCES

Memories I

Passing memory, imagined and intermittent. Memory like a chest of magical echoes, like a compass in a familiar closet. I graze my memory and shake her long locks of hair not knowing if I tell what I invent or if I invent what I tell. I wish to talk about a mythical and myth-making country, on the southernmost tip of the planet. It is called Chile. A fertile and generous land, it is a country of deluded wanderers and poets.

My father arrived here escaping from a Viennese cabaret dancer, and his brother arrived escaping from the gas chambers. I was raised in a very small town named Osorno, where I learned about the tepid rocks of the dawn and about the coriander and where I also learned that Jewish girls could not go to the German, English, or Catholic schools. Attendance, however, was allowed at the less prosperous Indian school where they learned how to love me and where I didn't feel like the "other."

In Osorno, Chile, the Nazis were the great feudal lords of the south and being Jewish was like possessing a savage and dangerous scar. I write these sometimes intermittent and true memories with the voice of an adolescent and then of a woman. I approach them, my memories, pulling out from my body a star of David and the Yiddish language secretly spoken in the silence of castrated faces.

In *A Cross and A Star,* I wish to talk about my life in an unseemly and noisy house in southern Chile and about a town with fifty Nazis and three Jewish families. Everything I tell you is true and this is why I write, so that it will be even more certain.

Memories II

So much humidity in the air, the rain with its luxuriant mantle of pain. The whole blessed day it rains between my vigils and anchored dreams, and I think about Anne Frank here in southern Chile, in Osorno, many years after the war. I am also thirteen years old and my name is Frida, the daughter of a man named Joseph, who came to this earth-shaken and generous country because he fell in love with a Christian dancer and that was his fate, the grand misfortune of the preordained. From Osorno he managed to save his mother and his brother and so many other Jewish emigrants who crossed the barbed wire fences in the fraudulent night and left behind the padlocks and the feathered quilts in order to come to this impoverished and humble country known as Chile, this southern land that taught them their first words of poetry and of love.

My memory, which is sometimes intermittent and fragmented, but always like an open canvas, approaches those frontier years in the south where the birds nest in immense skylights and where bread and food are the sacred rituals of the dawn.

I talk about what I saw in those years, I tell my story and that which was told to me by the foreigners who arrived at this lost and girded land between the Pacific and the Andes.

My Mother, Frida

My mother's name is Frida, which in German means peace. She is petite and quiet. When she speaks, I need only look at her ashen-colored eyes, the color of seaport waters, to be happy and feel those secret melodies of her inner peace. My mother is neither loquatious nor effusive; rather, she maintains a secret reserve and she approaches the gestures of love, song, and storytelling from many years' experience. Sometimes she takes me by the hand and I know that the moment of sacred memory has arrived. Then I listen to her and don't make any demands. I also don't ask her for details. I simply let her tell me things, like when the German girls in southern Chile snatched her dolls and made fun of her, or when they stoned her at the exit of the public school.

One day she wanted to tell her story, not because of a narcissistic anxiety to achieve immortality, but because it seemed beautiful to her to imagine a young girl of Viennese and Russian parents, living in the southernmost extreme of the world, learning the language of araucaría plants and praying in the afternoons in a hidden Hebrew tongue.

For a long time, I heard my mother tell me about the exploits of a childhood immersed in the sadness of foreignness and I gathered together her words. I didn't invent anything or perhaps I invented everything. Sometimes her voice rolls up like my own in order to confuse itself with the language of love.

My Father Joseph

The distant and very fine rain with its perverse monotony makes us foresee time lost in thought, like memory and voices that desperately play with recollection. In the rain-drenched nights my father would take out his green covered notebook as if it were made of fine foresty velvet and would tell us that only in the company of the dancing pines and the wise and heavy rainfall, could he dedicate himself to the act of writing.

None of us would approach his notebook that seemed travel-worn by the same color of the sea and its turbid green waters. My mother said that he wrote about his weariness and about the facial expressions of the dead and that with his hand he remembered the nameless bodies of his dead girlfriends because it was only out of love that my father Joseph came to Chile.

In Vienna of 1919, he fell in love with the graceful and bold legs of a Christian "goy" cabaret dancer. Years before the true massacre and shadow of the war, respectable Jews could not fall in love with Christians, could not attend public schools or play in tennis clubs; my father, nonetheless, fell in love with Magda. They said that her mouth looked like an enchanted bird, and maybe it is for this reason that he preferred listening to her sing instead of kissing her. Magda loved him with the strange piety and wisdom of women accustomed to that which grows dark and is foreign. Sometimes between songs she would hurl him a garter in the air. That was her sealed kiss of love, her pact with the foreigner.

His mother, horrified by the nature of this union, made my father depart Vienna and travel south. He crossed the ill-fated rivers of Austria. He more than likely traveled in one of those trains that would eventually transport hundreds upon thousands of terrified Jews to their untimely deaths. From Hamburg he traveled to Valparaíso in order to avoid being one of the so many incinerated bones in the forests of Auschwitz, in the hotels molded by wire and inhabited by the putrid excrement of human and noble life. He disembarked at the last harbor of the world, Valparaíso, a star-studded and intoxicated city. This is how my father Joseph came to the Chilean coast, fleeing love.

The Undergarment Salesman

In Osorno my father sold underwear, immense trousers that were not very desirable. No one liked those garments and would leave them on consignment so that the indigent could buy them at cheap prices. Since my father was an elegant and honorable Viennese gentleman, it was not possible for him to lie and he had to confess, because of his integrity, that his garments obstructed the physiognomy of the body. The years we lived in Osorno we were poor. I will not dare say happy, but rather poor and lonely.

Tailors

Almost all my great grandfathers were tailors, except for the less fortunate who were soldiers in the armies of Czar Nicholas. Some of them were landlords. That is, some enjoyed a special status since they already had a business under an umbrella where they sold droopy pants—clothing for the dead and the living—and used bridegroom suits on rainy as well as sunny days. Little by little these Jewish tailors gained recognition until they sent my Uncle Marcos to Buenos Aires to study and receive the first diploma in our family. In neighborhood Eleven in Buenos Aires, where Arabs and Jews still live, my uncle lodged at the home of our Aunt Adelina from Odessa. He suffered hunger and sorrows but finally managed to return home by crossing the Andean cordillera on mule, with a well-paying job and three precious bars of halva, that exquisite and delicious white chocolate, a true delicacy for the lips and palate.

That halva was sent by my Aunt Adelina and destined for Sonia from Odessa. Months passed and my uncle Marcos had still not delivered the halva. As you can imagine this irritated the families that constantly asked about it. I wonder what had happened to that piece of halva. What could he have done with it? Why didn't he drop it off the following day?

Three months passed and finally Marcos, along with my future husband, delivered the halva, but only two bars. Obviously he had eaten one, which made the family not only forbid him entry to the house, but also accuse him of being a thief, a bad tailor, and depraved person, all because he had eaten that deliciously perverted piece of halva. He was even denied retrieving his fur coat which had been left behind at the house when he delivered the by now notorious package. In a moment of insanity or boldness, they gave him back the wrong jacket of used lamb's wool and he never again recovered the respect of the family or that beautiful fur overcoat.

Raquel

My Great-grandmother Raquel, also from Odessa like my Grandmother Sonia, and a native of the same city, was fat and sweet. Her reddish hair looked like the smoke of a flickering and smooth flame. She was tiny and agile especially when she would begin to sing Russian ballads, imaginary balalaikas on nights of grief next to the late afternoon samovar, which would also confuse itself with her reddish copper-colored hair. Her fingers were long and slender, a reminder of the days in which she wrapped cigarettes and was happy. She learned to speak Spanish in Chile. She was fascinated by the melodic sound of Spanish words which she repeated with the accent of a Russian peasant even in her dreams, because she loved this new alphabet.

She learned to write in Spanish as well, and in a disorderly red notebook, she jotted down love stories about when my wise and crazy Great-grandfather Abraham fought in the Crimean War and she followed him to the trenches until she gave into exhaustion, thirst, and love in alien terrritory and in the deserts of an immense and lonely country. Raquel told about everything, remembering in her notebook when she worked as a cigarette maker in timorous factories, or when she arrived in Chile with her seven barefooted children.

My Great-grandmother Raquel told stories that were like distant things, like Mistral winds or the rhythms of sargasso grass. We loved her because she was generous and gave away money that she never had, as for example on holidays of happiness, like Hanukah. She would ask for a moment of silence and would donate thousands of pesos so that the poor could be buried. Once she donated an exhorbitant amount of money to educate the Jewish children of Chile. My great-grandfather accepted her mandates with wonder and speechless the next day sent a check for more than half the original sum.

Sonia Sofía

My Grandmother Sofía came from Odessa, the Crimean Paris. She spoke only Russian and liked to fall asleep smelling valerian drops mixed with tea, next to the samovar that she managed to bring with her hiddden in a green wicker basket that also contained two cheerful and lively chickens. We never discovered when she left Odessa and its sargasso shores. All we know was that she arrived in Chile by crossing the Andean range on mule with my grandfather, Marcos, an inveterate gambler and honorary Russian consul in Valparaíso.

My Grandmother Sonia arrived with her six children clothed with hides borrowed from muleteers who for a very modest sum of money, risked crossing impoverished wanderers and immigrants who arrived at the last frontier of the world searching for peace and a few coins to fill the emaciated bellies of their children.

My mother Josephina boasted about having been born

in Buenos Aires, the most European city of Latin America, although she never talks about being born beneath an immense frayed umbrella where my grandfather used to keep his scissors and needles, the tools of his trade, the only profession permitted to Jews in the notorious neighborhood Eleven.

My grandparents did not initially arrive at Osorno or other regions in southern Chile where Nazis, Indians, and Jews lived together. They arrived instead at the harbor of Valparaíso, that disheveled and untidy city shaped by elevators, flying brides, and dead people fleeing their coffins while mortals pursued them, collecting the evanescent shoes of the poor dead souls who rolled downhill.

It was on Ecuador Street in Valparaíso harbor where part of our family established itself. My grandmother was generous but had a dreadful disposition. According to my uncles, whenever her husband would arrive home late after playing cards, she would beat him with enormous copper dishes that the gypsies would sell her at a very reasonable price. She was a bit arrogant and whenever she would walk downhill to the fruit and vegetable market, the vendors would greet her by saying "Good morning, Countess." She in turn would smile back at them distantly and constantly recommend to them remedies for treating bad odors of the feet and other un-speakable zones.

I remember that on the wedding day of an uncle, in the middle of the altar, Sonia from Odessa begged the groom not to forget the Chinese ointment for control-ling spasms on his wedding night and that he also not forget the blue syrup for rashes and that he please wash his feet before tempting love.

Sonia was hardworking and dedicated to educating her children, the boys that is. She even sent the oldest son to a seminary. She didn't worry so much about her daughter because after all girls were pretty, quiet, and foolish. Sonia worked by selling tablecloths which she bought more cheaply from some nuns from Cerro Ale-gre, and she managed to educate her male children for professions never before dreamed of for Jews. Engineers and accountants were among them. When she had to pay for the thesis of her son, Gregory, the distinguished dentist of the Province, Sonia had to sell the red living room furniture, which she did without a gripe or sense of loss. She simply announced that no one sat in living rooms and that furthermore, no one visited the poor.

On late afternoons, during rare times of idleness, my grandmother, the countess, would sit next to her sam-ovar. She would wrap herself in a shawl made of smooth mauve-colored fabric and would begin to howl litanies deep from within. She would then sing or utter short laments like the music of lost things, like sounds of the earth or of absences. But always with the rhythm of a countess and the soul of a fine Jewish lady.

My Uncle Mordechai

My Uncle Mordechai Drusovsky was a student of the Talmud and he never worked a day of his life for anyone. He only dedicated himself to the obsessive study of the Talmud. However, he also had a restless hobby that involved scratching his ear constantly while he balanced the rest of his body with his sacred books. From so much moving and humming, he lost his balance one day and died with his ear in his hand and always listening to the language of God.

The Samovar

My mother's father loved his old Russia. In the late afternoons when the rain copiously slithered onto the sidewalks of Valparaíso, he would ignite his old samovar and cry about his mother Russia while he served us boiling tea with some odd cubes of sugar. Then, to finalize matters, he would play some Russian marches that were old like the furrows of his grief.

The Nocturnal Hip

My aunt liked the word for operating room, and the sound of knives in the hair-raising darkness of kitchens drove her crazy. More than anything she enjoyed thinking about surgical operations, not to put on airs or to feel a celestial alliance with medical science, but more than anything because it excited her to feel someone cutting her body into little pieces so as to later reconstruct it and find a place for all sorts of organs, loose bulges, and bones.

She wished for abdominal operations with even more intensity. For example, it greatly saddened her to not to have had her children by Caesarean section and to experience childbirth from the most beautiful depths of the stomach, near the womb. She envied those who had given birth by Caesarean and grieved that her five children had been born through the inferior labia of the human body.

Among her most memorable operations, she tells about the time they altered the position of her hip, almost raising it to the height of her chest and then with the not-too-familiar delicacy of makeshift doctors, leaving it right at the beginning of her pelvis so as to make it reach its appropriate and correct position. However, my Aunt Lucha lay prostrate because her hip had the bad habit of taking nocturnal strolls. It would slip from her body and liked to loaf about nude in the bathrooms and spend endless hours looking at the sky or pausing before the rhythms of the fierce and rolling waves. My Aunt Lucha begged it to return. Her wails were astounding and irate. My mother, who in that long ago time was a young little miss worried about menstrual cramps, went about the house like a lunatic looking for the mischievous hip until she managed to catch it as if it were a bold colored butterfly.

Aunt Lucha had fifty-two operations in her long life. When they operated on her internally, she also made use of the opportunity to ask the doctors to remove a callus. The doctors always feared her eccentric requests, but good-natured, she always insisted on the necessity of their removing every possible little piece during the moment of major surgery, which is how she referred to all of her operations, from the extractions of her blackhead to her open heart surgery.

Her last operation was perhaps the most savagely beautiful. They operated on the tendons of her left hand, cut open her abdomen, removed the gallstones from her stomach, and firmed up her breasts bewildered by so much life. However, she also insisted that they fix the big toe on each of her feet, and, of course, she didn't expect to be charged more because she still thought of herself as a Russian emigré in a land of Indians and Christians.

The day before her operation, she gathered together her twenty-four grandchildren and told them that she most likely would not perish, but that she wanted to see them so that she could smile at them the moment they brought her to the desired operating room.

She asked for brightly colored lights, she asked to see the intensely cleansed faces of the anaesthetists, she asked the nurses to wear crowns of geraniums because they were the cheapest flowers, and she begged the doctor to not use too much oxygen. While the chloroform entered her delicate, numb veins like pieces of blue sky, one could see that Luisa was happy in that mysterious peace of the sick and the dying.

When she awoke, she discovered that her toes had remained exactly the same. Infuriated she requested that the medical team meet her in her room. They obeyed but insisted that it was nearly impossible to agree to all of her demands in seven hours. But then the youngest and boldest doctor confessed to having repaired a minor callus. Luisa smiled once again, closed her green fish-like eyes and fell asleep because more than anything she liked to dream about living.

Washing Death

My Aunt Luisa used to wash the dead and shut their eyes on the thresholds of dream. She said that she loved them in a loud voice and she never repeated that sentence about how "the poor dead souls are blessed because their's is the kingdom of heaven." We Jews, that race which is always set apart, vulnerable, and persevering, didn't believe in heaven or in hell, not even my Aunt Luisa who thought that death was the opposite of life and that the dead were made up of tepid folds of open earth and that all things considered, the dead were not from heaven or from hell, but only from the earth itself.

Carmen Carrasco Espindola had different versions about earthly life and paradise. In spite of having baptized us, she was certain that we would go to hell. I thought about the powerful dimensions of a handful of holy water flung madly onto the forehead by a young and inebriated priest. Carmen Carrasco believed in the Holy Scripture, in the obscure music of the church, and in the poor body of Christ, disarmed on the altars, but she did not believe in baptized Jews. We Jews believed in covering the mirrors in order not to see vanity or anything resembling the human face in days of mourning. . . .

On All Souls' Day, as on Christmas, my brother and I considered ourselves diminished without history. Then Carmencita Carrasco, with her most Christian of gestures, would take us to the cemetery. But before, on the first day of November when they say that the dead install themselves on the Earth in order to eat their favorite steaks with french fries, that same day, she would rent a 1940 convertible taxi, which she filled with gladiolus and lilies. In addition forget-me-nots, a few fresh herbs, and little sprigs of mint were her offerings to the dead, and my brother and I would get dizzy with that sweet and perverse smell of flowers. The dizziness that overcame us was so great that we ended up falling asleep without even greeting or saying good-bye to a single dead person. This is why I think about the unsheltered body of Christ waiting for someone to kiss him and take him down from the cross. The image inspires me with a sense of wonder. I think that it is better to cover the mirrors, tear clothing as a sign of grief, and engage in acts of charity like my Aunt Luchita, closing the eyes of the dead.

Fox-skin Stoles

From the four families of Osorno, I remember Don Isaac inasmuch as until today he is the only Jew I know who still has not fought with God. He was boisterous and robust, he liked to pray in a loud voice and to beat his chest in mixed company. We respected and feared Don Isaac, perhaps because of his unkempt beard that covered him from his eyebrows to the moss on his ears. He liked to give us beautifully bound Bibles, and with those gifts we felt ourselves obliged to prayer and to perpetual obedience.

I remember Don Isaac not so much from his prayers as from his fur business and those strange foxes that he sold with the eyes of a decapitated animal. Society ladies would wear them amid the mist and during their late afternoon strolls. Those foxes were part of the dark fear of animals with faces of arrogant ladies that occupied my dreams and vigils. I also remember that on the counter of his store, "La Mansion de l'Hiver," was a solitary and lifeless mannequin leg that appeared in the dark, behind the mirrors.

I remember that leg like someone who thinks about love or its desires. I remember it with happiness or fear and miss it on warm days when the universe seems to shift like an abandoned time. Of all possible fears, I remember that leg with a silk stocking behind the store window in Osorno and I think about nocturnal houses, sleepwalking souls, the irascible night, and the sadness of lonely women.

Peletería L'hiver

Between the vigil that is memory, I am dazzled by the bright face of Don Isaac with that clearest of white beards that was more like that of Santa Claus than of a rabbi. Don Isaac was my Aunt Lucha's father who left Kiev at the age of twelve with his tailor's craft and a blood-stained thimble. He settled in Valparaíso, Chile, and discovered that he would find the happiness of love in those mad and unpopulated hills.

He learned Spanish together with the generosity of women as lost and as innocent as he, and he perfected his tailor's craft until he managed to establish himself in a brand new fur shop with a brand new French name, "L'hiver." There he presented sparkling and illuminated French models as well as a strange mannequin with only one leg and a brilliant silk stocking. For a long time, I began to understand what fear was, that delightful tickle transfiguring itself between pleasure and horror, that profound and tenacious palpitation.

For a long time I thought about the mannequin with the one leg and it sent shivers up my spine, but it also incited me to think about things that were associated with violence and love and to spend my life imagining women with decapitated legs, open and ready to penetrate the inclemency of ire, desolate and vulnerable.

Each time Don Isaac saw me through his shop window he would say, "Come here skinny little girl." He would then give me some sweets and teach me some prayers. When I was thirteen years old he gave me a beautiful Bible with a leather cover, and although I never read it I travel with it, especially on nights of love when the body is an open sacred zone. Then I think about Don Isaac, about his wise man's songs and his mannequin with the silk leg winking at me. This is when I caress the Bible without opening it so that I can rest.

Mrs. Valtiansky

Mrs. Valtiansky was an obsessive topic of conversation among the three or four Jewish families of Osorno. She used to wrap her head in a violet blue rag. She plucked her eyebrows and the hair on her ears, but the most incredible thing about her was that she like to walk around in slippers so as not to dirty the two frayed rugs of her house. They say that during the boat crossing from Sebastopol to Valparaíso, she only brought with her a veil of violet tulle and two rugs dampened by the tides.

From daybreak one could see Mrs. Valtiansky tie on her slippers and transport herself through her tiny house. She seemed to move about and fly with those same rugs that made her come to Osorno, Chile, the most remote place on the planet.

The Gold Teeth

In the afternoons when autumn was an immense blanket of yellow and crimson leaves, when we imagined that the earth was an immense trunk of noises and footsteps like the sounds of love, we liked to sit in the town square, Plaza Yungay, and see the lovers madly hold each other by the hands or eat roasted peanuts or recline in autumnal blankets.

More than anything, before the start of a luminous Saturday, we would approach Mrs. Spirman to gaze at her gold teeth. For years those teeth were the cause of many a sleepless night. Mrs. Spirman came from a small village in Poland named Jolem, where, according to my father, many lunatics lived because the inhabitants would marry among themselves and repeat the ancestral grief of a cautious pattern of Jewish intermarriage.

Mrs. Spirman says that she lost her teeth from fright when the Polish gendarmes entered her house and burned her recipe books and the Passover Haggadah. That night she became speechless, stopped eating, and drank only cod liver oil. During her boat crossing from Hamburg to Valparaíso they say that she fell in love with an amateur dentist and that while on the boat in exchange for love's alliances, he gave and fitted her with a bright set of gold false teeth that would shine in sleepless, moonlit nights.

The first time we saw Mrs. Spirman was when she got off the train that had come from Santiago filled with refugees scattered over the Chilean countryside. Her grey hair was tied up in a round bun, and as my brother and I gazed at our father extending her his hand, we saw those gold dentures throb and shine in the darkness of that fervent afternoon.

Before the Sabbath, Mrs. Spirman approaches the plaza and kisses us, and I keep silent especially when she shows me with so much faith and passion those gold dentures that preserve a history of generous journeys and fruitful loves.

Superstitions

Superstitions were the daily rituals of my Grandmother Sonia, not only on days of thirst and death when the mirrors were covered and the disfigured face of pain left the body and soul. The countess, Sonia, had stored in all the corners of the house a handful of salt and sugar and a candle to illuminate us from evil omens and to fill us with human life. She never allowed us to leave our shoes and hats on the beds or our wallets on the floor because this is how the money would run out.

For good fortune in love she recommended garlic and an elixir of anise and for foot odors she always recommended rinsings with boiling cauliflower water. What we didn't know was that when the countess was successful with her sales of tablecloths, she liked to consult a fortune-teller named Olga Tolchinskaya who dressed in long plushy black garments and painted her face in an exaggerated manner, looking like a haggard old witch.

Olga was not an expert at reading tarot cards. The figures on the cards frightened her and she thought that predicting the future was closer to the sense of touch and to a kiss than to the images on these ancient cards of chance.

In the evenings, when the grief and stupor brought on by anxiety were enormous, like still untold stories, Olga and Sonia would take each other by the hand, close their eyes full of legends, and reminisce about Odessa and Leningrad and the immense nocturnal fire. This is how they remembered fear and when they looked for Jews in the granaries, kitchens, and squares they would embrace each other tightly and think about the safety of a possible future.

Olga could never invent omens because all she had

to do was caress that sunken face of the countess to prepare her for the avatars of her fate.

Good Omens

Only on rare days of happiness when her digestion followed its path and the fish chosen by the "marquesa" Sonia were very fresh would she devote herself to giving us advice and competing with the herb doctors who lived further downhill.

She told us that for love sickness one must rub two cloves of garlic in the chalice of the left inner ear, and for foot odors, one should apply an elixir of tigerskin and lentils before midnight. In order to fight against the traffic of sadness, one should forget the word *pogrom,* forget the fire, and hide the Star of David deep within the fearful and moaning breast.

Eva

Among all the voyages and exploits, my mother remembers when she crossed the Andean range on mule. The muleteer sang when the night became deep and strange, when fear penetrated the souls of the travelers through the biting cold snow and raw mountainous winds. My mother spoke of all this next to the stove and flickering flames, pausing before each gesture and statements filled with sighs and cadences.

My mother told us that when she followed her own mother to Bolivia, to the city of Cochabamba, the desert wind whistled agonizing and entered through the skin's pores molding our jaws with dust and words. The high plateau was a precipice of moons and the silent landscape filled with careful footsteps as the wind cut through the rhythm of the air. It was then that my mother was pregnant with Eva, who was born in La Paz and died ten days later. They buried her in a little white coffin that looked like it was made for carrying dolls and angels, and they wrapped her in newspaper while my mother looked out at the desert wind and gazed at the tightness of pain. My mother looked at that little white coffin, those newspapers, and the Jewish cemetery on the high plateau; an imaginary abyss.

Tattoos

My girlfriend's mother has a tatoo on her arm that is tinted and sometimes can be confused with a faded meadow. She doesn't exert the slightest effort to hide it, and the curious ask her when she had it done, if it was an act of will, of fellowship. She looks at them satisfied with their blessed ignorance. They are for the most part peasants from the farmlands who have never left Chilean territory and for whom the word *Jew* sounds as strange as words like *Treblinka* or *boutique*.

My girlfriend's mother doesn't talk about trails of death or about the war. Sometimes she says that bones remind her of doleful sheets and sedatives of terror. Sometimes she cries, although she acts as if she cannot cry and very softly repeats that what pleases her more than anything else is being alive. Then I notice that she always looks at the sky which she says she sees covered with smoke and pain.

My girlfriend's mother has a tatoo on her left hand, and it seems that she came to love it as I love my scars and the things that are confused with fortune and grief.

The Door

Like other members in our family my husband's father was a tailor. In the old country he bought a door that served as his workbench during the day and as a warm and generous threshold at night.

Liesl

Of all the stories, of all the unspoken silences, I remember the story about my Aunt Liesl as if its words were recently lifted from the sea and similar to beginnings.

Liesl lived for a while in Prague, and at the beginning of the war she traveled clandestinely in those nocturnal trains until she arrived at the border where she then crossed the English Channel on a small, obscure boat. She said that she couldn't look at the sea at that time because they carried her wrapped in thick and dark shawls.

When she disembarked at the port of Arica in northern Chile, she took a humble train from the saltpeter mines that brought her to the city of Cochabamba, Bolivia. Suddenly, in the solitude and nostalgia of the high plateau, she heard a voice calling from above and saying "Liesl, Liesl." It was her father creating signs and gestures of love from the desert.

It was on that voyage from the Atlantic to the Pacific where Liesl lost sleep over the extraordinary sea. It was then in those illuminated crossings that she discovered sexual urges, love's throb, and the men who looked at her from afar on the deck, with the certainty of a glance that penetrates and excites. Liesl, in those crossings, learned about desire and sex sweetly warming her young body.

Trains I

My father did not like to mention trains. He remembers the squares of Vienna, of Salzburg, and those of Prague where the trains would turn off to carry animals and Jews. My father quivers when the whistle of the irascible train enters through the glass panes of our house. I, on the other hand, dream about mute and dark trains with cars filled with food and sugar. I dream about slow-moving trains that will carry me and my Grandmother Helena through beautiful landscapes and pastures, trains that will not carry us to the cupboards of death but to a brilliant dawn bursting with life and color.

Trains II

At night we recognize the brusqueness of the sound, the arid and frayed earth calling us. At night Jews dream about trains, about doors that shut tight and about a world that hides itself so as not to see them get on those ocher-colored trains, those trains destined for the crematoria.

All the blessed and clothed night, Jews dream about trains, about the dryness of the forest, about sealed prison-like doors.

If you would only embrace the darkness, you would see the human flow whirling about among night's dreams and you would be caressed by their luminosity rising from the excrement.

In nightmares, Jews dream about train stations floating in the mist and about doors shutting against the ashes.

I dream about trains, about that savage moan, about that harmful geography of war.

Ana

In the beginning of the war and in particular when Hitler annexed Poland and Austria, my father actively worked to rescue his Jewish brethren. Since there were only three Jewish families in Osorno, my father traveled to Santiago in a dilapidated slow train and journeyed next to the shadowy faces of that affectionate and damp land, which he learned to love more than anything else.

In the capital he became associated with an organization called the Jewish Federation of Santiago, which in the years 1938 and 1939 had only fifty members. My father's responsibility was to receive those Jews destined for the province whose first stop was our city of Osorno.

Many times my brother and I accompanied him to the train station where we would meet them. They arrived pale, with a worried gaze and a look of fright in their faces. They had no belongings except for a few cracked wicker baskets and traces of solitude in their eyes.

Sweet Ana Morgenstein arrived on one of those

trains. She cried because her sister Hannah had been sent to another southern outpost in a country estate beyond Osorno and close to Puerto Montt, and she thought that they were once again separating her from her loved ones, as they had in those furious days when her mother crossed the death line and entered the blue gas chambers of no return of a disgraced Germany.

My father embraced Ana and presented her with a bunch of recently cut copihue blossoms from the mountains. He brought her to our house where she lived for many years. She taught us German songs and at times we would see her gaze through the windows in the afternoon, looking at the emptiness toward the forest, beyond the fields in search of her dead mother.

The Montecino's family from the ancient Chilean upper crust and practically the proprietors of all the country estates of Osorno hired Ana as an instructor for their children. They wanted her to teach them strict German discipline and the wisdom of Goethe. However, they also obliged her to hide her Star of David and her past and they changed her name to Fraulein Douglass. On Sundays she could be seen attending mass, but they never convinced her that Jews have horns in their forehead.

Ana always continued being a Morgenstein and like a good Jew she also continued fighting with God.

The Have-Nots

In times of scarcity and oblivion, my father, with his charitable works, worried about burying the dead and paying for the voyages of as many Jews as was possible to save. My father was only interested in human life and for him that was being a kind Jew. My mother, on the other hand, was both practical and primitive. She wanted us to have milk and tomatoes and trips to the shore once a year. Around that time she decided to record in a ledger all of the excesses of my father. She wrote in it the cost of the burials, the cost of the charitable under-takings as well as his scarce appointments with love. This is how she developed the habit of charging my father for every extra breath he took, for all of the extra showers, and for all of the "have-nots" he had so gener-ously helped. My father died with an enormous deficit, but he managed to continue to bury the just of the town with the money that he left behind.

The Pink Cots

Since we were very poor but dignified, my mother used to comb through the hospitals in search of beds that belonged to the dying. At home she would then paint them pink. She not only worried about Jaime and me having a place to sleep, but she also had various cots in the living room for the terrified emigrants who arrived at our house on the corner of Yungay Square next to the enormous shade-bearing trees.

Misty Letters

Of all my mother's secrets, the ones that most incited my curiosity were the love letters hidden in a satin sky-colored suitcase. I never could catch a glimpse of their content but I do remember having seen the careful calligraphy that adorned their envelopes, as if all passion and human discretion were subjected beneath those very beautiful letters that irradiated calm desires as well as tears and distant smells.

I liked to look at the inkwell, the blotter, and the special pencil—now forgotten and obsolete objects like that secret and hidden box where she kept all of her desires. I remember that once she told us that she had received a letter written in blood. My brother and I looked at each other in amazement, and we were terrified by the thought that those luminous letters could have been written thanks to an intrepid knife that cut the fingers of some fond and vindictive lover.

My mother told us that the letter came from the saltpeter mines in northern Chile and that it was written by an old Viennese suitor who liked to sign as

Romeo Weiss and who would perfume his letters and kiss them, dying them scarlet. When my mother stopped answering him, Romeo sliced his finger and smeared it with radishes, although the evil-tongued say that he spread it with his mother's accursed eggplants so as to fabricate his blood letter, his legacy of love, soaked in the passion of the flesh and of vegetables. However, according to my mother, that reddish letter eluded all notions of war, all signs of violence and merely manifested a delicately perverse scarlet-colored calligraphy, imploring nostalgias.

Births

The pregnancies of my mother were legends, scraps of life, of that which could not be, legends blackened in coagulated blood. She had three children and five miscarriages or deaths, minute and immense sorrows. Her body was orphaned so many times, cut and opened so many times. On the days of agitated blood, the sorrow was like a deep lock that lay buried inside her body overflowing with life.

Her fifth small and immense miscarriage occurred in 1949, the first time that snow had caressed the rooftops and streets of Osorno. The children, lovers of the transparency of that which dazzles, went outdoors to conquer the privileged space of whiteness. All this happened at dawn when she bled copiously like a young maiden in a tale about wicked witches and stepmothers. In the immensity of the whiteness itself, the Chilean Red Cross ambulance arrived and two men with massive black capes picked her up. All this occurred on that beautiful and terrifying snow-covered day, on that day in which the black capes of death-like smoke, carried her to the antechambers of life.

Aunts

Between dreams, above and on top of them, beneath the secret images, all the piercing looks, all my dead aunts with their dislocated ears, with their veins pulsating with the terror of rage, appeared perforated on the Sabbath tablecloth. My grandmothers and their grandmothers were spread apart and opened like deformed blood clots. I always dreamt about my dead in the dining room of the house in Osorno while the Jews talked in a sickly German language that robbed the sleep of precocious and perhaps innocent people. All the blessed night, I was with my dead, in step with the Sabbath candles, and I asked a deaf and mute God why he let us be burned in the ovens fired by rage. I dreamt that I was the one who went with them aboard the trains of evil madness.

Nena

One of my father's brothers married a Christian, or goy as we called her in my family. She was skinny and arrogant and wore an immense black cross around her neck in order to fight against her remorse for having married a Jew as well as to assure us that it was our fault that Jesus Christ was hung from the bare wood and died from the cold. Despite her gaze of sorrow and amazement, she turned out to be a perversely interesting individual with her black silk stockings and her pointed witch-like shoes. When my father died she decided to make a bonfire of memories by burning all the photographs of the Russian ancestors and thus trying to eradicate all the evil spirits of the Jewish race. She hung her cross from her neck and I saw black doves adorning her flaccid hair.

My Grandmother Sonia from Odessa, c. 1924.

Sonia in Odessa around sixteen years old, c. 1904.

Sonia and her sisters, Olga and Emma, Odessa, c. 1902.

Sonia, Marcos, and their children: Josephine, Raquel, and Goyo, c. 1918.

*Don Isaac with his wife Rebecca and their children,
[my Aunt] Lucha and Gregorio, Osorno, 1937.*

Josephine in Buenos Aires, c. 1923.

Josephine and Joseph at their wedding in their home,
Palacio Polanco, Valparaíso, 1926.

In Osorno
rain dwelling
in the crevices of sleep
tinting the restless pollen
of the night.
rain,
in the obscurity of fear itself
singing the gestures of
every forgotten sound
and my mother,
waking
tied
to a vegetal clamor:
to the music of rocks
and memories.

IMAGES OF MY YOUTH

The Siesta

We played in the dark rooms when our parents huddled up, would sleep the unpardonable winter afternoon naps. We used to see them from behind the beds, swaddled by the mahogany wood like two darkened mounds. We loved the silence of the house because through it we could imagine the presence of bats and birds of evil omen. My brother would often hide beneath the bed and stay there for hours, waiting for the exact moment in which to strike, while I, also lying down, would cut out remote and disfigured pictures of old movie actresses.

Just as I was drifting off to sleep, he would jump, raising and shaking the feathered mattress, and I terrified, thought that it was only the beginning of the end of the world. Now I remember him buried beneath the earth knowing that his movements would be imprecise and distant like those of a child approaching his own death.

We enjoyed playing hide and seek, but above all, we liked opening the closets because people said that they contained skeletons dressed in red and resembling the dead. Instead we found elegant figures with dresses of silk organdy like those for First Communion, dresses that little Jewish girls were not allowed to wear because they were the daughters of the devil with horns in their foreheads and tails in their behinds, because they possessed the scent of sacrifice and sadness.

Beds

Extraordinary beds in their magnitude, occupying the round spaces of their chambers, looking out toward the sargasso sea or toward the fleeting faces of death.

How they hypnotize me by their arrogance or benevolent humility! There I touch them, calm or restless, awaiting the return of the bodies that will disrobe and desire each other in the plenitude of the flesh, in order to rest, to sleep, to love, and to prepare for the final breath.

Beds make good hiding places for people like my brother who liked to crawl underneath them and scare me in the dark rooms of the house by dressing up like an obscure gentleman and rocking me from the most remote place on the floor.

I remember the bed made of oak and beech wood in the house in Osorno. It was small and maintained the appearance of savage wood in its contours. In it I would dream about shadowy zones and would think about how exquisite it was to lie down and plan for the following day, to pray for my great grandmothers, to prevent the next earthquake, to pray for my mother, my brother, and my father who, above all else in the world, loved Sunday afternoon naps.

My bed in Osorno, like a furrow in my memory, is where I learned about accumulated grief and about the little bodies of lonely people. My bed in Osorno is where I prayed for the end of earthquakes and for my relatives burned in the obscure forests of Germany.

Thresholds

My brother and I would approach bedtime when darkness summons indifference and distances and the fear of evil things appears behind shattered doors. The evening light would invade us like a sinister mirror-studded blanket and I would want to pray to the little angels. I imagined them with the freckled faces of little German girls. When I wanted to say, "Angel, sweet companion of my defense, don't ever abandon me at night or during the day," I wished to think that that winged figure would come to cover my feet and whisper to me that no one would kidnap me in the roundness of sleep itself, that angels also protected little Jewish girls, that men were noble, and that everything would be mediated in heaven.

It was that night when the noises seemed like swords that were close by, when all of my dead grandmothers were resurrected in the barbed wire camps, when I was afraid to open my eyes and I began to pray the way I had heard the nuns pray in the nearby school, and I felt that the little angel that approached me wasn't a man but a wise woman without a cross and without black stars but simply something resembling the sonorous wind with its enormous wings protecting and covering me.

Fears

We liked to feel fear like a sweet gush of air releasing itself along the sides of the stone house. We liked to feel the wind making orgies out of words. Then in the dark heaviness of the night, in the circles of terror, we went over to the home of the Saez family, the owners of Osorno's funeral parlor, a progressive family not very fond of nuns and Germans. After all, they were socialists.

My brother and I enjoyed these visits because death at their home was a feast, a type of eternal nuptial, a game of sunflowers and challenges. Sometimes we closed the boxes and loved all the silence and peace of those vulnerable characters sleeping in a coffin of evil death. When I now think of coffins, I realize that we loved life too much with its luxuriant mornings near the woods and that we never thought about that unspeakable lyricism of the black boxes. My brother lies in one of them today. However, I remember nostalgically when the two of us would embrace next to the coffins, defying the waves of death and eating with the dead.

Childhood Dreams

In my school my friends talked about heaven and about a man with immense wings and enormous purple keys who would open his legs to let the good girls pass through the thresholds. They also talked about eating the decapitated and fragile body of a man who was tied to the cross with a look of supplication and terror in his eyes. They told me that Jewish girls would never reach heaven's gate because they were dirty and virtueless. I only remembered my aunts Estella and Helena nude in the forests of Germany, thrashed by the brutal barbed wire fences.

When they forbade me the entrance to heaven, I invented a paradise on earth. I imagined it as a blue blanket of very fine threads. I imagined a paradise filled with railway cars and whistles like the ones in the movies where women and men tenderly bid each other farewell on the platforms.

The Christian heaven didn't interest me. Instead, on hallowed and starry nights resembling miraculous chicken pox, my brother and I would invent our own sky. As we gazed through the forbidden attic window, we were happy like the children in tales filled with cotton candy dreams.

Cucumbers

When I was a young girl, my mother instructed me in culinary matters. She told me to take a cucumber from out of the grocery bag, but many times I would bring her a green squash or a bunch of juicy radishes instead. I thought that cucumbers had a lot to do with little green squash, and since it was so difficult for me to distinguish between foods, I decided to write stories, giving myself the opportunity to lie. Who said that cucumbers are green?

The Ladies of the Night

When my brother, Jaime, and I returned from school at the dangerous hour, that is, when the sun dazzled us with its lukewarm rays and amorous colors, we liked to stop by the Office of Sanitary Inspection where the beautiful and delirious prostitutes would await the weekly inspection of delights and rites of love. I was fascinated by their fishnet stockings and their high-heeled red shoes and swore that from then on I would always wear a pair of red high heels before making love.

The Chocolate Tree

As a young girl I always believed that chocolates and not only fruits and flowers grew in the luminous crowns of the trees. In the days preceding spring when the rural roads in southern Chile were no longer solitary but covered with poppies and lavender and the meadow was a festival of roses and hollyhocks, my father would return home through the fields somewhat disillusioned in his unsuitable occupation as an itinerant salesman. He would stop at the modest wooden houses outside of the town to buy us homemade chocolates, and very early at daybreak he would hang them from the flowering trees. At that time the four Jewish families of Osorno didn't feel so desolate and would celebrate spring along with us beneath the golden wonderment of chocolates growing in the beautiful tree tops.

Bread

Very early in the morning we went to pick up fresh bread at Doña Blanquita's. However, before arriving at her house that resembled the generosity of her hands and clay ovens, we had to cross a vast meadow where the sky confused itself with the sea and where the noise of emaciated dogs traveling in small packs and dark and shallow pools covered the plain.

We were afraid of crossing the meadow, we were afraid of our passing bodies breaking out in sweat while we ran in the morning darkness.

At that time I would embrace the bare legs of my brother, his sweat would diminish my grief, and the drowsiness of the smoke would appear between my hands. Our fear was both pleasant and disquieting. We looked at the meadow and listened to its howling herons. Someone in the distance carried fresh fish and cherries on his shoulder. Then and only then, my brother and I knew how happy we were together. Then, in the fear of darkness and light, we huddled together embracing to pick up the bread.

The Sea

My brother and I had never seen the sea. We lived in Araucanian territory, on the fortieth parallel that is Osorno, a region like sargasso water, hollow and rainy. We imagined it copper colored, perpendicular, and in motion like leopards watching over their new packs. Sometimes, when the rain made silent puddles on the skylight of our room and when the cemeteries filled up with larks, we would dream about the sea so that we could cover our extravagant and awkward nudity with that sumptuous body of water.

On the day that my grandmother, Frau Helena, announced the arrival of her ship at the harbor of Valparaíso in 1937 we discovered that we would finally see the sea, incandescent in its splendor.

All night my brother and I huddled next to the warmth of my father resembling embers of tenderness. That train would not ultimately carry us to the gas chambers but to the blue of the Pacific ocean and into the arms of Frau Helena.

My grandmother arrived from Hamburg Harbor together with her son, Mauricio, on September 18, 1937, Independence Day. Valparaíso greeted them with its wilderness of hills and simple flowers in clay pitchers.

My father, impatient, rented a small launch so that we could reach the ship more quickly.

How much I loved the silvery waves made by the boats and how much I fell in love with that incandescent smell disturbing me and filling me with such good omens. And the sea was there, with its winding coastline, happy like the color of love.

There we saw her standing and reassured, wearing a silver fox stole on her shoulders and delicate gloves of white lace. That was my Grandmother Helena with her hair arranged in a bun and wearing a hat of blue tulle. Her face was covered with a veil that moved in the breeze, transforming her with its fluctuating gestures. When I saw her she kissed me as if I had also come on that voyage with maleficent foam and a war helmet. She spoke to me in the related languages of German and Yiddish and she carressed my forehead asking me if I also loved the sea.

During my solitude and exiles, I like to approach coastal cities that smell of seaweed and algae, where I devote myself to finding old grannies with hats made of blue tulle because in each one of them I see the face of Frau Helena. I also remember the first time that I, the young girl Frida, approached the sea in order to embrace her grandmother who had survived because the

Germans could not take her away, because her eyes were emerald colored like the waves, like that which illuminates and flourishes. Since she survived, her body is also of living water.

Coasts

We used to go to the coast looking for fireflies and their rituals of funereal dawns. We went to lose ourselves in the spectacle of the day and of time. At daybreak we would comb the shores searching for agate stones that looked like the hair of ancient and disheveled ladies.

My parents and my brother and I would walk along the coastal route of Angaroa where we would pause every late afternoon with the intensity of children astonished from looking at the perpetual sunset on "princess rock." According to legend, a Mapuche princess fell in love with a white man and hurled herself into the sea in despair. This is why on nights with a full moon it is possible to hear her weep and to see her grieving face on the rocks.

Toward the Splendid City

When we were young and still full of the dream of a new dawn, we crossed the city with that smell of daybreak and stones and someone between the silent distance and the first lights of an uncertain fog shouted at us: "There go the Jewish children," and the stones of darkness filled us with spilt blood, blood storified and confused.

Spirituals

The virgins had little blue eyes and rose-colored cheeks. They looked like me. I believed that they were Jewish angels but unfortunately the Jews don't believe in angels or in crucified gentlemen, least of all in virgins. How much I would like to have had my own Virgin so that I could go and visit her on Palm Sundays, to make her promises and votive offerings and kneel next to her rosy feet that were not blue from the cold, as Gabriela Mistral would say. Jews believe in invisible things, in a God whose name cannot even be pronounced, a fearful and threatening God. When men visit Him they cover themselves with enormous white and celestial prayer shawls. They move to and fro as if they were rivers and from very deep within their soul, they smile. But it is difficult to believe in that which cannot be seen, to pray in a low and anguished voice. Catholic girls cover themselves with tulle and incense. In their pockets they keep spirituals of golden angels and blonde young ladies breast feeding the Christ child. In my pockets I only keep a few stones to protect me on the way home, just in case someone calls me a dirty little Jew girl. I will never carry with me spirituals of good angels.

The Virgin Mary

Among all of the little virgins I preferred the Virgin Mary because she was like a member of my family. She had blue eyes, was blonde haired, and they say that she was the mother of a Jew named Jesus who was crucified by those of his own blood. This is why they say we Jews are bad because we ate the entire body of Christ with his little blue eyes.

Atheists don't even pardon him, but all things considered, have the Jews been pardoned for anything? Did God pardon us when we got lost in the deserts of Egypt or Mesopotamia? Did God pardon us when He led us astray to the cobalt ovens?

I like to argue with God. I fight with Him and believe that He isn't everywhere because if He were, then why did He abandon my Aunt Alma dead in the invisible hallways of Poland? And why does my father have numbers marked on his soul?

The wise man of the village, Don Isaac, my Aunt Lucha's father, assures that only good Jews argue with God. I fight with Him frequently and the matter of fasting does not please me in the least. Besides I have seen my mother eat a clove of garlic behind the door on the Day of Atonement. I understand her; in her situation I would do the same. Perhaps I would eat a leg of smoked pork, but never on the Sabbath.

I think about God a lot but on the nights in which I imagine that we will have an earthquake or lunar eclipse, I don't pray to Him. I merely tell Him to be alert to so much calamity because if He isn't, that means that He isn't everywhere because if He were, the little German girls would not spit at me and would not call me a dirty Jew.

Coffins

In the beginning of the month of September when the light filtered itself through the shadows of the funeral parlor, the grandparents of Raquel Saez removed the coffins for spring cleaning. These coffins for the dead were sad and solitary but never gloomy. They had remained empty without human life for more than six months. I liked to climb into one that was plush and velvety like the case of an enormous guitar. Raquel would bring drinks for us and for the dead and bread crumbs so we would never lose our way back to the light. Within them, she and I would embark upon long discussions about life and death and would talk about the smell of moss in the children's coffins.

After an intense dialogue, we would say good-bye to each other and cover ourselves with crystalline shrouds. Then we would happily and fearlessly slumber into the coffins of dreams. We slept this way until the light of the following day would wake us with all of its fragrances, with all the happiness of beginnings. This is why I could always talk to my dead, to my Grandmother Helena from Vienna and to Uncle Isidoro from Malmo. However, I can't seem to find the face of my brother in the mirrors and now I regret not having read him more stories while his open heart still lived and pulsated.

Words

Ever since I was young I liked words, those that had certain rhythms and elevated cadences like the word for firefly, *luciérnaga,* or the word for clairvoyance, *clarividencia.* Sometimes I repeated them loudly or in the solitude of my room of fibrous wood, and my nanny, Carmencita, would twist the corners of her mouth while hearing me. There were also certain atrocious words like the word for scar or for calvary, or words that alluded to menstruation. The word *uterus* affected me with terror and desires or, better said, evoked a great sluggish nostalgia between my legs, always closed, always sealed, always panting and reserved. However, when I heard the adults talk about the foreskin or the penis, I suffered from a subjugating sadness. At first I thought that it had to do with wanting to cut the throats of certain little marine animals. Later I understood that they were talking about my brother and the ritual of circumcision, a pact among all Jews. Being Jewish seemed to me like something that conjured up blood and knives that had nothing to do with fish or with fat women.

Among all the words, it is true that I like the sound of the word *alliances, alianzas,* mother's favorite word. But upon hearing talk of foreskins I tremble from cold and nausea. At these times, I wish I had a cross.

The Goys

My father did not like us associating with goys, not because of some particular prejudice, but because of an old fear of the paranoic, of the persecuted, of the survivor. My scarce friends were from "the colony," with the exception of our neighbors: the "urgent" young ladies, called such because whenever they knocked at my door they would say "urgent." My father would not let us participate in the goy holidays or Easter. He said that it was the black dream of the Jews. However, New Years at the sea was another matter. My brother and I left the night before for Valparaíso and the following day, from eight o'clock in the evening onward, we gathered at the harbor with Jews, Moors, and Christians and my fat aunts.

Valparaíso was an immense illuminated flower, unruly, solemn, and beautiful. The boldest, kissed each other half-nude beneath an accomplice moon and we only looked on, although we always maintained a discrete distance beween who they were and what we were, Jewish children isolated from the grand commotion of the human race.

Valparaíso

Valparaíso, restless and neglected like a conceited woman fond of her blue strands of hair confusing themselves with the mirror of the sea that is simply a fragrant piece of sky. After Osorno, we moved to Valparaíso where my father worked in a German chocolate factory named "Hukke." From distant and rainy southern Chile, we arrived at this mad port of the Pacific where self-admiring sailors loafed about the docks greedy for love, and where Rubén Darío discovered the color blue.

For many years we lived on Echaurren Street, next to Don Isaac who moved from Osorno with us. In that city of the Pacific, we were the first Jewish family in the central zone and my grandfather, a distinguished gentleman and nocturnal gambler, was the honorary consul of Russia. Until today my family still lives in central Chile and our surname is well known, perhaps because we are vendors of automobiles and jewels and because we are also astute in matters of business.

Christmas at the Sea

We liked to spend the month of December in Valparaíso. I remember that on Christmas Eve we would timidly approach the house of Manuel, the gardener, in order to bring him a small Christmas gift: money, wrapped in shiny paper. He would invite us into his home and would offer us cakes and red wine in immense glass bottles. Above all, he invited us to look at his beautiful Christmas tree decorated with some enormous and marvellous cherries hanging and overflowing in their redness like the delights of life. He also gave us a bouquet of fresh bay leaves tied to a red carnation foretelling good omens.

The Burial of the Firemen in Valparaíso

Every summer my brother and I took the night train from Osorno, bound for Valparaíso where my uncles, aunts, and grandmother lived. We boarded the train on a star-studded night, shining like the Southern Cross. The air grazed us with an almost magical litany and my brother and I swelled with pride seeing so many stars in such a very small country. One time, after traveling a few hours, the lights dimmed, the train's whistle sounded as if it were saying good-bye, and we slept embracing one another until we arrived at the bustling and disheveled city of Valparaíso.

My Grandmother Sonia, the "Countess," waited for us at the station, but before arriving at her house on the steep and poor hill, we would buy fresh bread and fish, necessary foods for good-mannered young people.

During these three months we would sunbathe on the sidewalks or go to the swimming pools together with my aunts and uncles. My mother was terrified of rickets and this is why she saved up the entire year for our summers. She wanted the sun in our bodies and the sun in our dreams. Among the many memories of these visits that I keep like obsequies of time is the day the firemen were buried.

Firemen aren't just anybody in my country. They aren't merceneries of money or of fire either. Being a firefighter is a serious matter. One must demonstrate professional and moral integrity but also have a bit of bravado and, above all, pride. Firefighters put out fires thirsty for love, and they don't receive any compensation, only the bewildered looks of ecstatic children and of trembling women, mad with happiness. For them dying is as important as life itself.

From my grandmother's house we could see all the buses, bicycles, caskets, flying brides, and the dead dancing through the hill on their way to the neighborhood cemetery. The dead firefighters traveled along the same road, happy in their luminous coffins. Once the police had cleared away the traffic caused by the few remaining automobiles and by the "micros" which descended with names of women: Rosaura, María Celeste, Juana Manuela, and Teresa María, all blowing their horns with some half torn and bright flags waving, the firefighters with white pants and blue jackets began to file by, each holding a candle in his hand and loudly repeating the name of the deceased while the night resembled a blanket of fiery stars looking splendid and noble.

We would get scared watching those burials. Sometimes we looked at the sky with terror because we wondered who would put out the fires of the wooden cliff houses with so many dead firemen. Sometimes we asked ourselves why Catholics used so many candles to remember the dead. In my home we only covered the mirrors and my grandparents beat their chests.

The whole blessed night, my brother and I stayed on the street corner, watching the last procession file toward the cemetery as the lights of Valparaíso went out like someone blowing out the candles of the last birthday cake. In my lapses into insomnia, I remember the burial of the firefighters and dreams of evenings and seaports.

Christmas Times

During Christmas we felt strange and anomalous before that commotion of gifts and huge old Santa Clauses sweating in the summer heat of the Southern Hemisphere, dressed in reds that resembled anger more than love. My mother had the custom of giving the maids of the house thimbles from Vienna and tape measures calibrated in inches from England. This is why the sewing they did for her turned out to be so obsolete and strange, with enormously wide shirt sleeves and very long hems: gringa clothing.

My father would tell us that Christmas was the beginning of the dark night for the Jews and that comment disturbed me, since my brother and I already looked at the sky as a blue expanse filled with things resembling angels in love. Looking at the sky on summer days was like looking at eternity and paradise, but we Jews did not believe in that eternal life or in the transfigured soul or even in the colors of love and charity.

When my friends talked about the son of God and Heaven I felt an enormous desire to be a Christian and to also have my First Communion all white and winged, but more than anything I envied those prayers in which the children were assured that a guardian angel would protect them. My nights, on the contrary, were inhabited by incinerated grandmothers, barbed wire fences, and screams where no one paid attention to the voice that implored the right to asylum.

My father said that Christmas was the night of the broken crystal and I didn't understand what he was telling me until I figured out what his words meant whenever they called me a dirty Jew and Christ-killer.

Nevertheless, I like Christmas because I can see a fatman sweating in the middle of the Chilean summer while I eat a juicy peach.

Not All Trains Are Sad

My mother used to say that not all trains are sad. Some bring us to the seashore and recede from the perfidious smoke of the cities; they descend through the intrepid foliage of the forest and make voyages a furrowed spectacle beneath the confines of memory.

The happiest train of our childhood was the one that would bring us to the Pacific coast, to the strange port of Valparaíso where the houses seemed to have sprung up haphazardly. We traveled from Osorno to Valparaíso, and a few hours before arriving, we could already experience that impassioned fragrance of the sea breeze, that swift conjunction of algae and seaweed. At that time my brother would embrace me and would begin to take off his shoes, anticipating the sensuous texture of the sandy beaches. I, in turn, would prepare to gaze at the immensity of the rocks and faded bathers. But more than anything, what I carried deep within me were those eternal nights of insomnia, when I thought that the trains would also carry me to the platforms of vague blue death.

Carpentras

My father often spoke to us about a sky-colored synagogue and I thought that he was probably rambling with words from heaven. Synagogues are usually not elegant and were less so in ancient times when everything was forbidden to the Jews, especially elegance.

However, many years later I managed to become acquainted with this celestial synagogue in the little town of Carpentras in Provence.

The synagogue is the oldest in France and has a sky-colored ceiling, the color of love, the color of God and of children. One needs only to look at its dome and abandon the celestial shawls of the ceiling to touch its rounded happiness with a gaze and on tiptoe.

The ceiling is celestial blue because in the fifteenth century when the wise Jews wanted to build a school, the monseigneur refused them permission and the Jewish children were left without a place to study and learn. The monseigneur was afraid that the Jews would become educated. Therefore during a night of misfortune and sadness, the wise men of the village decided to paint the ceiling blue so that the children while praying and laughing could touch true happiness.

Frida, age three months, 1929.

Frida in Valparaíso, c. 1932.

Joseph, Frida, Jaime, Josephine, 1937.

Frida with Jaime and Josephine in Osorno, c. 1940.

The small boat that picked up my Grandmother Helena in Valparaíso, c. 1937–38.

My Grandmother Helena's first Passover in Chile, Osorno, 1938.
In the center are my Grandmother Helena and my Grandmother Sonia.

OSORNO

Frida

I was always fond of deserts because of their captivating and heartless solitude and because of those shadows that stretch out wide and empty on their expansive surfaces. I was born in northern Chile at a time when it still belonged to Peru. I was born in Tacna but lived for a while in the Bolivian city of Cochabamba where the air pierced through to our bones and filled us with the certainty of our own mortality. In the streets they called me a "cholita" instead of a Jew, and being compared to an Indian or a person of color was a capital offense in spite of the fact that I was blonde and had the face of a cute little porcelain doll.

We lived in a very poor and dilapidated house whose walls seemed to deflate pendant upon the kindness of the whimsical wind currents and because of the dirt-floor, on cold nights the hard earth felt like my mother's cracked breasts toughened by the many agonies which filled them.

Since we lived very close to the cemetery, we could sometimes see the cactus-adorned funeral wagons carrying the dead to their new dwellings. According to popular belief, on certain nights of sublime enchantment it was possible to see some blue fumes escaping from the graves. These vapors, which probably arose from the heat of the minerals and the saltpeter, gave the graveyard an eerie look which frightened us and kindled our imaginations, conjuring up images of ghosts and goblins.

When my dear sister Eva died from diphtheria, they buried her in the cemetery of the blue fumes with only a Star of David and the solitude of the desert caressing her. When she died my mother knelt on the ground, tore her garments, and groaned about her fate with the grief of her ancestors. It was then that my father Joseph decided that it was time to leave behind the sadness and return to the south.

We crossed the high plateau on a sickly mule until we reached Valparaíso and from there we set out for southern Chile and to Osorno where I grew up and was happy and where they no longer called me a cholita but a Jew instead.

Daybreaks in Osorno

Women selling bread arrive at the door smelling of smoke and coriander leaves. They seem to have come cascading from the geography of the cities and they seem to have escaped from my mother's story where they were never mentioned but converted instead into invisible ladies of the morning. However, there they were, selling loaves of braided bread. Not having eaten themselves, they arrived meticulously fulfilling the schedule of the bread and of our holy days.

Not only could I see them from my room but I could also smell them arrive with their shawls curled up by the frost and with their hands that looked like furrows of earth. My mother timidly received them in the doorway and they left behind their gifts in the territories of the palate and of life.

I see them glide through the frost and confuse themselves with the grey grasslands of a winter that becomes and expands. Innocently, they approach the house of the German family and I motion to them with my lukewarm hands that become soft and warm with the unadorned bread of the grateful.

The Araucarías

We entered deeply into the forest because it had clearings and poppies and we liked the fragrance of wet earth resembling the bodies of women who love. We descended behind the slopes, along the ridge of branches and recited, inventing the names of the leaves, of the trees submerged in the deepest araucaría groves. Sometimes my brother and I would undress in the forest, remembering the nude women in the German woods. However, in this forest in southern Chile, there was no smell of smoke and there were no golden and grey barbed-wire fences. We liked the forest because it was savage and tender, because the nocturnal animals were no longer there and everything was very clear and diurnal like floating aromas, with the wind protecting us from the bark and the omens of abandoned children.

Sabbaths

The darkness whistles as if it were the heels of a lonely woman. In the distance the darkness begins to kindle like a silk tablecloth and four families of the village arrive on foot to celebrate the sacred ritual of the Sabbath. My mother blesses the splendor of the Sabbath from a table tottering as if the millenary spirits were balancing on it, and she prays for the missing, for the persecuted, and for her incinerated sisters. Someone knocks at the door and they tell me that it is God's wind, although it turns out to be another new emigrant who recognized our house from the tenuous light of a few loving candles and from the smell of freshly baked bread filtering through the doorway.

My School

In Osorno there were only three schools, that of the Carmelite nuns who chose the faded color of dry earth to protect themselves from the evil spirits and who covered their necklines with heavy linen fabrics. There was also the tidy and well-maintained German school where they still kept a picture of Hitler in their most sacred vault and where the teachers spoke German in a sharp voice as if the words themselves were lacerated blows, as if the sound of each syllable were violent and malevolent. In addition, in the outskirts, near the beginning of the woods, was the public school where the Indian girls, natives, and orphans went. I was a curly-blonde-haired Jewish girl like those who appeared in the spirituals of virgins, like those who appeared disheveled in the German camps, like the German jailers; I was also blonde and remote, belonging to another culture and way of life.

MARJORIE AGOSÍN

The German Catholic girls didn't want me in their schools, so I went with the Indian girls who arrived barefooted and blue and purplish from the cold and who repeated, "Blessed is the kingdom of the poor." They accepted me and crowned me a princess. In the mornings they combed my golden and wavy hair and made crowns out of dry copihue and eucalyptus leaves. In the afternoons they accompanied me to the corners of the squares because no one permitted them to enter the city, and this is how I would return home with them on late green afternoons. I returned knowing that in their school they wanted me, that in an Indian school a Jewish girl was welcomed.

We loved to cross the clearing in the forest with its smell of pine trees. We imagined ourselves as beings composed of verdant materials and illuminated aromas who had left the earth behind. We liked the forest because beyond it was the school of the English girls who had emigrated because of lost chastity. We heard them sing in a strange and familiar language, in a speech similar to the secretness and divisions of elegance. When my brother and I returned from the school of the poor, of the natives, and of the sparse Jews in the region, we would lean over the school wall to hear them sing, and in the lullabies at midday they sang: "Who stole the loaves from the oven? Who stole them?" and an emphatic and enraptured chorus would respond with "the Jewish dogs." Miss Wilkins, the principal, applauded and smiled. She wasn't German but an Englishwoman who also rejected us even though her good manners concealed her contained anger.

That horrible and melodious song clung to our necks, to our bones, and to the root of our memories, and on days of dread a ravenous and evil voice sings within me about how the Jews not only killed Christ, but also rob bread from Christian ovens.

We never again crossed the forest on the road to Union school. We preferred the solitude of the return trip home, with the rain creating furrows of kindness on the faces of two confused children of Osorno, a region of foreigners, Nazis, natives, and a few Jews.

In my school of little Indian girls and poor mestizo children where grand events and transgressions did not occur, everyone possessed a gaze of sublime obscurity. Every Monday we sang the national anthem and we prayed to the Christian God for the welfare of the school and of the Inspector General. I was the only one who asked God to avoid earthquakes. One day they announced the visit of Gabriela Mistral, the renowned poet of dark skirts whose countenance reflected the innermost being of the silent children. Señora Gabriela, "Aunt Gabriela," would come to the school for a few hours. Since I was blonde and didn't look like a little Indian girl, they asked me to present her with a bouquet of flowers, shifting and luxuriant flowers that looked like the waves, southern, reddish flowers from the end of the world. That day I let my hair hang loosely and listlessly. I looked like a girl from the German school although I knew that they had chosen me because I had a passionate face and they thought that perhaps Aunt Gabriela would have liked to receive flowers from me. Then I approached her. It is true that she was ugly but she smelled like the earth and had an appearance that was sublime yet sad, evoking deep, untouched sorrows. I will never forget the time I presented Gabriela Mistral with the bouquet of wheat and fresh flowers on behalf of the school children from Public School #3. She embraced me and I hold within my gaze her hands of water and the warmth of her poetry like that nebulous way of understanding sadness.

Gabriela Mistral

I still don't know why the teachers chose me to present Gabriela Mistral with the bouquet of roses and violets on the day that she passed through Osorno. Some evil and perverse tongues said that it was because Gabriela Mistral liked Jews, that she wrote about the Jewish people; others, the more innocent, said that it was because I was a sweet little blonde with little blue eyes. Then I looked at them with a nostalgia that was vague and distant. I only thought about how nice it would be to wear a dress made of blue percale and how I would loosen my hair to recite a poem of hers. But it wouldn't be "Los piecitos azules."

When Gabriela Mistral arrived the school became solemn and silent. She had green eyes and a displaced gaze; she wore a long skirt and men's shoes. I approached her and gave her the bouquet of freshly cut flowers. And she kissed me on my cheeks drenched in sweat and shame. From that moment on I loved her because everyone also laughed at her and called her a dirty Jew, an ugly lesbian, and friend of the unfortunate Indians.

Years later I learned that Doña Gabriela was a teacher to my aunts in Temuco who belonged to one of the oldest and most distinguished Jewish colonies in Chile. Mistral talked to them about love and about the Jewish race; she gave them a sense of belonging in a sacred history and she spoke to them about usurped identity.

Puerto Octay

Puerto Octay was one of the first German colonies established in Chile around the year 1855. It is approxiamately an hour from Osorno and presently resembles certain phantom towns of the desert where sadness is the shadow of the concealed. Then Puerto Octay was a site of privilege, with huge wooden mansions and salamander stoves that emitted an aroma of tepid wood and peaceful homes.

I spent two summers in Puerto Octay at the home of two German girls who were my friends. Since we had much in common and perhaps because we were blondes and light-skinned, it was possible for us to get close although they never knew that I was a Jewish girl.

To reach Puerto Octay it was necessary to travel through a huge stretch of muddy and rocky terrain. The road heading south was blue and the mist seemed to rise from the earth. I arrived at Puerto Octay captivated by so much beauty. It was in the summer, the time of watermelons and love. My body also blossomed to the rhythm of that natural world with its alchemies and fragrances of wood and savage things.

My second summer in Puerto Octay was drastically different. Upon entering the main door of the house, I was confronted with an extravagant and huge portrait of Adolf Hitler situated on a small altar of lilies. The mother of my girlfriends prayed to Hitler like someone praying to a savior. At that time I was thirteen years old, and I used to hear the emigrants tell stories of terror and agony in the living room of my house. Without saying a word, I fled from my friends' home disheartened by the knowledge that I would never be visiting them again.

Dignity Colony

Since the forties in the south of Chile, some seventy kilometers from Osorno where the thickness of the forest immobilizes the vision and the verdor permeates the body like a somniferous balsamic, a mysterious colony with the sinister name "Dignity" has existed. It was suspected that malignant Nazis, sickened from wrath, arrived there to die beneath the placid foliage of southern Chile. It was also rumored that personalities like Mengele hid within the vicissitudes of Dignity Colony as well.

Admittance into this colony was absolutely prohibited and from afar the arrogant German flag could be seen waving in its perverted history. The peasants of the region, who were the employees in charge of keeping the grounds clean, cutting the grass, pruning the perfumed roses, and maintaining a perfect order, would hear the frightening howls of children flogged in their transparent nudity. For years no Chilean government was able to gain access to this sinister colony. However, in the seventies rebuffing suspicions and inquiries to the contrary, the astute Germans opened up a tea room serving perfect strudel and concealing the traces of death behind the sinister thresholds.

The Feathered Blanket

We liked that restless hour in the late afternoons when we would celebrate the colors of the forest and luxuriantly reach the light, tenuous and dispersed, in the transparent thickets. We liked the times when the clarity foretold a serene darkness and the trees also seemed to open themselves like enchanted mothers who arch their arms in order to reach love which is a perpetual root.

My brother and I didn't follow a fixed course, we simply wanted to leave Osorno to feel ourselves inexhaustible and to breathe the air that was so ours, so deep and sweet from the almond trees.

We were like the beginnings of rivers, like the beginnings of love, nude in all our innocence. There we would stroll along the river's bed, waiting for the arrival of the white herons who would occupy the widest and most obscure extreme of the forest. As we gazed at their silhouettes, they filled the woods, the world with a dream of white feathers.

We liked the forest, the herons, the feathered blanket.

Joseph

My father says that believing or not believing doesn't matter; what is important is speaking with God.

French

In Osorno, the rain with its lightness and misty garments. My brother and I would spend solitary hours and days anchored to its tenacious melody, to its sounds against the wood and against the canopy of a disfigured sky. Sometimes we thought that somewhere between the rain and near the cemetery, our dead grandmothers would return together with our Aunt Adela who knew French, an exquisite language forbidden to the Jews of Vienna. At those times we thought that they would return and that they would bring us apple strudel.

My mother says that she never found out about the fate of my Aunt Adela, who was asked to appear at police headquarters one day. She went with her French books and a fashion magazine under her arm. That was the last time my mother heard her sister pray in French.

Aunt Luisa's Beauty Pageant

When Luisa won the beauty pageant she paraded through Osorno's pebbled streets with a red velvet dress and a yellow dragon incrusted on her left shoulder. Luisa Smirnoff, with her green eyes and reddish dress, resembled a turbulent queen illuminating the very small and wise Jewish community. The spectators greeted her with golden-colored confetti, rice, and bread crumbs while the Germans were preparing to boycott the triumph of such a beautiful Jewish girl with a red dress like a flaming talisman.

The afternoon in which Luisa was queen for the day in her native town of Osorno, the Germans were preparing to vote for Hitler, their favorite candidate. At that time they headed for the sea on express trains and in small and obscure vessels. They went in groups of five to vote on the open sea for a foolish and heartless dictator who adored music and the blood of Jewish children. My beloved Aunt Luisa, who today washes the bodies of corpses, was happy for a day. Her breasts swayed next to the dragon and the red of her gown and her gaze was a carpet of vivid dreams.

Banisters

Grief or what they call sadness enters through the banister. Grief like a very slow melody of goblins resembling a hoarse solitude, enters through the soul's spheres. Grief for not being able to be like them and to wear starched dresses like those worn for the First Communion and on days of love and festival. Grief for not wearing bluish crosses and not believing in the amulets of angels.

We are people, Jews persecuted by grief, not for any political idea but only for the wild chance of having been born wandering Jews, with a tatoo on the soul and sad protruding eyes with scars.

The Nazis

In my country they protected Nazis who arrived with official passports from different embassies. Sometimes the resident German colony would wait for them with flowers and Wagnerian music and I would think about that girl named Anne Frank who resembled me with her braids, that girl who rode a bicycle and liked to collect prints of famous actresses. The German colony, with its cortege of Nazis, was respected. We Jews, on the other hand, were only allowed to devote ourselves to commerce, to the tailor's trade, to sewing on buttons and praying in the dark.

We never occupied prestigious positions and we were not permitted to enter the armed forces that continued that detestable goose step march, and continued giving orders in German . . . and intimidating the soul. When the war arrived they would kick my cousin Moses, my future husband, in the halls of the university. The Arab students with noses so similar to our own, would also hit him for being a Jew and spent much of their time mistreating him. At that time, he had a knife that he used for autopsies and with it he defended himself cutting the faces and the brows of the unwary.

With the passage of time we resigned ourselves to living with this hatred. We knew that in Osorno the German colony had enormous and beautiful dwellings and that they celebrated their magnificent parties of the New Year with Wagnerian music. We Jews who didn't have clubs or nocturnal celebrations, looked at them from afar also resigned to a remote time and fate. And the little Indian girls watched those enormous blonde men and women who said they recognized us from a distance, and the German girls spit at us behind the illuminated windows. I remember all this on New Year's Eve when the Jews would take refuge in the empty clubs while the poor and foreign children would play hopscotch like someone wanting to trap heaven and earth between his feet and heart.

The South

Night and its presence of rain like a watchman of sounds, like a caretaker of the rhythm of the trees. It is through the rain and the thickness of the fog that I return to the south as if to a distant time of sweet love. I return to Osorno as if finally rediscovering that space where I learned about processions between the mist and about the sound of the rocks and mud between our hands.

I approach the moss and stumble upon small rivulets drenched by the frost, and there is the door with its enormous copper and bronze padlocks that brought us to discover a place beyond the light and there is the window that made us feel the perverse innocence of children who know how to look and be seen.

The house alone, uninhabited with that smell of time and moistened history. The furniture like deflowered fans and between the cracks, behind the thresholds I see the faces of my mother and of my dead brother.

1993

Southern Chile stretches out before my gaze like an intermittent and sacred landscape. The long expanses of earth sometimes acquire ingenuous and dreamy forms for the navigator. My country is a blue strip of land resembling the fish of the earth. I tremble going through it conserving that subtle poverty of the humble folk who still remain within their brightly painted homes that emit grey vapors of coal and dignified misery.

I travel through southern Chile at daybreak looking at the reddish and golden dawn like a sunflower where women with bird-like voices forever appear in order to sell fresh bread, beef jerky, and whole milk, a milk that is fertile and foreign to the pain of barefooted children who perpetually plod along trying to learn to read.

In the late afternoon, I go to Plaza Yungay where I used to swing with my winged dresses. The yard of my house is now a corner grocery store but I still see it resplendent with chickens and herbs. How much I have won and lost in my voyages! However, above all else I maintain my language and the capacity to be astounded before horror. The garden of my house is like the heart of a savage girl.

I walk toward the center of the city and there before me is the German Club where they would let my father, the Jew, enter only after lunch hour. The ritual repeats itself. I appear suspicious to them even though I am blonde. My eyes are too defiant, I smell like the poverty along the public roads and they don't permit me to enter.

This time I walk as if nothing could astonish me

and the feeling of being violated from everywhere is so immensely familiar to me. I walk through Osorno and see the same men of the war years, this time more robust and doleful, darkened by their bureaucratic suits. They savor their German language and treat the Indians of the south with the same insolent arrogance of before. Osorno continues to be invaded by generations of Germans and Nazis who have not yet learned to appreciate the tolerance of the Chilean people. Besides their sausages and exquisitely well-maintained homes, the legacy of the Germans in Chile is almost null and void.

I walk along the sidewalks of this provincial city. It is summer in the southern hemisphere and the smell of peaches, fruit, and wild flowers stretches out like an inexhaustible tablecloth of human life. The people in the street: the vendor of herbs, the knife sharpener, and the organ grinder with the little parrot who supposedly assures us of good fortune, still remain witnesses of a life whose past is an extended and tranquil time.

It is Sunday and the sky seems to fill up with balloons. I am in love with the light, the air and life. This time no one persecutes us and the war years are like a disfigured silence. In the distance, in a strategic place in the city, I pass by the German school building where thirteen-year-old children like me would file by a huge and perfidious swastika. Today the firefighters of the German Club repeat the same ritual.

When night falls and it seems as if southern Chile were filling up with the shadows of birds, I walk through the streets of my childhood again and think that I still have a country to which I can return and call my own.

It was here that I learned to look at the strips of crimson sky and here where my father would go to the train station looking for those made destitute by the war, bringing them white shirts and bright bouquets of copihue blossoms, the national flower of Chile that is found amid the mountains and snowcapped peaks.

Dazzled and lost as if blindfolded, I find the roads that will take me to my house, my garden and orchard. I stop before the beautiful antique shop because I am reminded of the porcelain dolls that my Grandmother Helena hid within her trunks. I enter the store as if treading through a narrow pass and I am confronted with immense portraits of Adolf Hitler. The man says that they are very popular, that the Germans in Osorno still are accustomed to hanging them on their walls. He suggests that I look at them up close, that they are authentic. He talks to me about Adolf Hitler with an enthusiasm and spectacular passion that frighten me. My blue eyes look at him anxiously with that millenary fear of the Jews. I imagine that my head is a blazing forest. I imagine myself bald and boneless without eyes. I imagine thousands of pitch-black jail cells and a universe of deep walls without an exit.

Osorno of 1993, how little you have changed. Antique dealers continue carrying their most prized possessions in their shops: portraits of Adolf Hitler, and I, terrified, go out to look at the birds of Chile, the storks and the thrushes, and I see my father waiting for the last train. . . .

February 1993

Raquel's indistinguishable house is located a short distance from the municipal square. I come to visit her by surprise, even though she intuitively waits for me with our favorite welcoming food: empanadas and a dark thick red wine. Raquel embraces me and leaves her crutches leaning against the family piano. Then I remember when they shouted at us: "There go the cripple and the Jew." I remember the voices of the children in the German school who wanted to hit her for being lame and for having a Jewish girlfriend. I also evoke the memory of my Aunt Luisa who was her best friend and chose her as her lady-in-waiting for the impoverished beauty contest of the province. The unusual spectacle of a cripple carrying a Jewish girl's scepter of orchids was as memorable as that clamor of broken glass in the funeral parlor the following day.

And here we are as if time had stopped on the peripheral beauty of a coffin. Her living room is spacious and silent. She, herself, reminds me that it was here where we would play inside the coffins arranged according to their social class. The coffin lined in red satin occupied a tier of extreme importance in the living room of the funeral parlor and the one adorned in poplin, a lesser spot. The ones without a lining were for the peasants and political prisoners. . . . Who said that death makes us equal?

Raquel, with her slow-gaited movements, tells me that this Osorno is just like the one that existed in 1938, that there are still large Nazi enclaves, that in many sectors of the city only German is spoken, and that Germans still don't allow marriages of impure blood with Chileans. There are still shrines for Hitler and I tell her about that young German fellow in the antique shop across from the square who offerred me a picture of the Führer at a good price.

Osorno appears before my gaze like a great nocturnal mirror. I advance along its paths and tremble before the familiarity of that which no longer is. I step into the mist and from afar I perceive volcanoes, fog, and clouds of smoke. I dream about Osorno as if it were changeless. I dream about the thresholds and my mother's hands celebrating the harvest with clusters of golden wheat.

I have dreamt about absences and about trains void of fear. Only a whistle in the terrifying night makes me relinquish my skin and memory. The pain increases as in births, tearing and mute. In the distance a bandurria bird sends me a signal with its multicolored music.

Last night the stars formed an enormous branch of blue lights and behind the windows, the first view of my town appeared looking at me as on that day in which I went to the school of the Indian children and they kissed my hair.

I think about my country and it hurts me. It is a borrowed region of vast plateaus, knolls, and snow-capped peaks. Nevertheless, I sleep and tremble within it, unable to avoid it. I love it and shiver in its kiwi and peach fragrances. I am a knoll of rubble before its majesty, round like a womb foretelling good luck. From so much pain and happiness, I immerse myself in my country and become again that little girl lost on the southern frontier. My return journey is also like a train advancing in the darkness.

Sitting opposite aged memory, I approach and care

for it; it is a passing and intermittent music, a circle of red flames like the tousled hair of women in love. One day I began to listen to my mother and she told me about her years in southern Chile before and after the Second World War. Bewildered, she told me to tell her sacred and dark, painful and stirring story.

For a long time I approached her words, like warm blankets and dangerous roads. Sometimes their silence made me stop before the proximity of horror.

A Cross and a Star relates the personal experiences of my mother. I gathered them together, made them speak, arranged the episodes, and transformed myself into a thirteen-year-old girl from a province in southern Chile surrounded by Nazis, Christians, and native inhabitants from the region. This is the story of foreigners and exiles and it doesn't matter if I forgot your name because you are also in the dark dwellings of memory, crossing the dangerous thresholds of all bygone times.

Osorno

I

I traverse
the cities
of the Nazis
where only Jews
and the children of Jews
lie buried
singed in sleep-drowned acids
waiting for the
malefic, mute trains
with other Jews inside
with nude Jewish women
curled up in the mist of fear.

II

In the Nazi city
vultures of life
scenting,
a glory resembling the evil omens
of dead birds.

III

In Nazi

cities

Jews,

amassing dreams,

making plans

alliances.

Trees in springtime, Osorno, 1970, oil painting by the distinguished Chilean painter Sergio Montecinos, whose sister, Marta, married Mauricio.

Osorno, near the center of town, 1990.
Photo by Luis Ladrón de Guevara.

Etelvina Cuevas in Río Colorado, c. 1967.

Etelvina Cuevas with her daughters,
Rosa and Marisol, 1972.

Helena and Sonia, 1944.

CARMENCITA AND THE KINGDOM OF ADOBE

Baths

We loved the kitchen with its enormous wood-burning stove where we ceremoniously performed the ritual of our weekly baths. My brother, who always had grafts of earth, lizards, and eucalyptus in his hair, went first. Carmencha eagerly would throw wooden sticks under the unsteady and restless caldron and only after the water would make strange gurgling noises would we begin to enter the balsamic power of its tepid depths. In the distance, very close to the pantry, my mother would observe us. She always had an absent look about her and seemed like a lonely princess watching two savage children submersed in a grimy tub.

Carmencha would tell us that we should hurry to

frighten away the always present bats that lived in the rear of the house, and we would only think about the next week's bath and the enormous caldrons of water. Our red and sweaty faces would drop into the profound sleep of children or insomniacs. Only then did I discover that my body was unlike that of my brother, filled with soft, docile, and smooth protuberances, shifting in step with the water's movements and to the rhythms of a flesh resembling sponges.

I wasn't afraid to look at myself because the rippling water elongated my forms and made me grow. Underneath the water I imagined a kingdom and a home without a leaky ceiling and without bats where the sun entered with rage, where the rain was merely a Sunday diversion, where my chores included reading stories to my brother, and where by looking at myself in the mirror, I could pretend to be a princess, distant like my mother, imagining happiness in a bathtub.

Blue Kitchen

The smoke entered flurrying through the blue room. Carmencita Carrasco liked to paint the kitchen in a shade of bluish blue not for reasons having to do with calm or melancholy but because she assured us that those colors drove away the flies. The thick mist of things at rest and cooking, the gigantic pieces of chicken, the profound sweetness of oregano and parsley, filtered through the terrifying and dazzling kitchen. The doors remained hermetically sealed because of that terrifying fear of air currents, which according to Carmen Carrasco, made the mouth sag and the neck permanently bend making love become a lament resembling the sadness of bereavement.

Filling ourselves with the luke-warmness of fear and delight, we would prepare to listen to her tales of ghosts and of princesses kidnapped on Saint John's Eve, on enormous white horses with two heads. There was a fireplace in the kitchen, restless and bare, making swirling noises similar to the sounds of birds and swallows. And there was also the never absent shared mate, to kill sorrows, accentuate deliriums, soothe the heart, and cure the misfortunes of love. And all of us, my sisters, the maids of the block in the obscurity of the blue room, with that half sharp and hoarse voice of Carmen Carrasco summoning the ghosts, the dead who floated scorched behind the earthquakes of Chillán, were numb with fear, a fear that made us slumber off to sleep to the vapor of the beautiful things. Sometimes Carmen Carrasco would pull out a chicken leg from among the bubbling vapors of the pot, and we would all chew on it together, ignorant of what are called foreign microbes, of colds bewitched in the delights of phantasmagoria; together we were submerged in a blanket of smoke, in a breath of mist, and the voice of Carmen Carrasco continued rocking back and forth like the deep rivers, like mirrors that end up tossing out our soul.

The Banquet

Carmen Carrasco Espindola would invite us to the most glorious celebrations in the kingdom of Osorno. Among her guests were my mother's neighbors, the four Jewish couples in the town and sometimes my aunt, "the Hungarian," a name we had given her because of her devilish disposition and reputation for reading cards in order to drive away good fortune. One night when the Hungarian arrived we knew that there would be a scandal because Carmencita Carrasco always served her the smallest drumstick on the table, the most insignificant piece of pork, the tiniest slice of roast beef, and, of course, the oldest sprig of parsley. The Hungarian cursed her and I crossed myself beneath the table and prayed to the good Star of David that my relatives would act discreetly on the nights of Saint Carmen.

Baptisms

It was a savage and sleepy Sunday. They woke my brother and me up as if they were going to bring us to the treasure islands or to tell us soft and perfidious secrets. Carmen Carrasco dressed us in our ironed and starched outfits and my reddish braids glittered in the early morning light. Before the enormous stone house showed signs of stirring, she brought us to church to baptize us because she feared that horns would otherwise sprout from our forehead. I bowed my body and head and let that lukewarm water resembling urine reach down into the depths of my soul. I also winked at the priest who had fearless blue eyes and felt myself overwhelmed by a strange form of happiness. I could now finally confess my sins and enter a perverse, dark room where I could talk loudly about the delights of carnal love.

The Cross

Carmen Carrasco told us many things, some very loudly so that the women of the neighborhood could hear them and others, in secret. For instance, she told us that now that we had been baptized, above all, we should follow the example of the Lord Jesus Christ who was crucified and died for his goodness. She insisted that we had to be like him. While she looked at us sweetly, she crossed herself and proceeded to put pieces of potatoes on her forehead to protect herself from headaches.

For years I believed that if I were not good they would crucify me, and it terrified me thinking about spending the nights awake and tied to a frozen wooden cross. Perhaps it is from then that I acquired the legacy of being an abstainer before God and before the terror of coagulated blood. Perhaps from that time I preferred the Jewish religion at all costs, because the destiny of our Lord Jesus Christ tied forever to his cross didn't seduce me but rather caused in me a profound sadness, like the sadness of wells and dark city squares.

Carmen Carrasco

After the dawn of the earthquake in 1930 the entire city of Chillán looked like a cemetery of the dead and the living, a real mixture of bones and corpses, only a howl of voices resembling a pack of hounds more than the sound of relatives entangled in those bundles of skin and bones. Carmen Carrasco spoke with the dignity of those who suffer and of those who love. We listened to her, shuddering from terror, and we felt a fear that was infinitely delicious.

Carmen Carrasco arrived at Osorno in one of those

trains that the government provided to help relief victims. Among her only possessions was a chicken, Daniela, who had stayed tangled in one of her shawls, thus avoiding being split in two by the treacherous rubble of earth. She also carried with her a handful of salt, a candle, and sugar, the only elements necessary for survival and for making a home. With her belongings she ended up at the hospice of Holy Savior of the Tomb Hospital where she was able to rest, shut her eyes, and learn to pray for the living.

Her prayers were composed of a perpetual melody and rhythm that awoke the interest of Rosaura, our washerwoman hospitalized for an infection of the jaw even though she barely talked. The two discovered each other to be wise and generous. Rosaura offered to share her bed with her in the small room in the back of the house of her employers, but Carmen Carrasco, with her usual generosity, asked her instead for a job.

I remember that Carmen Carrasco arrived in the month of September with her crimson-stained, bandaged arm and with some strange cigarette butts resting against her temples. At that time spring began to unveil itself and signs of happiness and of colors, like greens and yellows, began to appear along the countryside. Carmen curtsied before my mother, and she in turn remembered her first kiss on the hand by her husband, Joseph. It was then that she decided to accept her as a maid. However, both women came to love each other, to share memories, and to mix country herbs with Jewish recipes.

Carmen Carrasco lived with us for forty years. She protected me from evil spirits and from cadets, she was my confidante, she kept my lipstick hidden in the wooden electrical meter, she waited for my late arrivals next to the fireplace, and her hands slid over my skin practicing an exorcism that resembled matters of happiness more than of demons.

Carmen Carrasco protected me from love sickness. With her by my side, I learned to dry herbs and to convert them into special remedies used for curing ailments. I also learned to thrash trees on Saint John's Eve. Furtively she brought my brother and me to the town church, and with holy water she frightened us about evil omens. This is why she preferred to save me and carry me in her lap to the thresholds of a religion that I also loved, because I liked the sinister peace of the candles and the smell of death from burning incense.

Shawls

At dusk when the sky seemed like a veil of microscopic stars, we approached her small room always situated near the corner of the kitchen and dark zones. There she could be found in her roundness, bound to a toasty warm coal-burning stove with tenuous flames that reminded us of rituals and phantoms. She wore her familiar shawl, lead-colored and tattered by the many years of pleasure that had given it a color resembling life and the earth.

My brother and I entered her room and snuggled next to her smelling of cigarette smoke. We liked her pock-marked skin resembling dreams and children's illnesses that store and gather the secrets of sickness.

She also embraced us and we remained together in the disquieting darkness for a long time. Mama Carmencita was wrapped in her old, threadbare shawl. She placed little pieces of crumpled cigarettes on her temples and fine-tuned her voice like a doleful knife in the immense night as she prepared to tell us a very long and delicate story. She always began by telling us that we should preserve a respect and silence for the storyteller because if we didn't, her words would turn into black birds.

My brother and I also embraced each other and listened to her, silhouetted by the smoke and spellbinding words. We would fall asleep next to the coal stove, next to the cracked walls in the room of Mama Carmencita, the servant of my parents and of my Grandmother Helena, who was for us a light amid the mirrors of war.

Carmencita

Carmencita Carrasco appears behind the night with her enchanting scissors cutting scraps of life and making curtains resembling rainbows and incantations. She likes percale, poplin, and cobalt blue linen cloth and makes us clothes for traveling in imaginary and imagined carriages as she covers us with shawls to astound us before love and its splendors. Carmen Carrasco's clothing drapes itself over her tired body after sleep and long walks. We still preserve the red and greenish curtains, the shawls, and the apron filled with corainder, and sometimes when I am sleepy, I begin to dream about that wardrobe that protected all of my gazes, that helped me in despair and filled me with sunlight and clarity.

Carmencha Carmencha

Carmencha Carrasco liked Saint John's Eve because in the immensity of the Chilean sky and beyond all human frontiers, it was possible to invoke the spirit of the dead, making Hector, her son lost in the earthquake, approach to kiss her on the tip of the nose and making the night a pool filled with magical wonders.

On the eve of the hallowed night, Carmen Carrasco would give herself a long bath. She perfumed herself with mint leaves and sprigs of anise and at this time would remove the potato peels that she always wore between her temples to cure the evil eye and fright.

My brother and I would accompany her to the countryside where she would thrash the trees in order to summon fertile growing seasons. After repeating the exorcisms of the night, we would go to her room in the most remote and dark corner of the house, where we would bathe in a festival of transparency and light. All the candles, all the tomatoes and oranges were placed around her beech wood bed. Then we would look at each other before the mirror and she would swear that she could see the shadow of death forecasting good luck.

Gazes

Carmencha will not stop looking at us; her eyes are like two strange, sharp-sighted fireflies, those fireflies that only shine with the arrival of the dead. It is so strange for me to see her squatting next to the water. I see her toss away some herbs to cure love sickness and I watch her prepare a potion of nuts, raisins, and meat juice, curled up and lost in her woolen shawls, soaked by a long sorrow resembling innundations and earthquakes.

My mother often tells us how Camencita lost her son Hector in the earthquake of Chillán when the earth constricted. It divided in two, creating fissures in the sidewalks and clouds of dust and awakening even the irascible dead. Wrapped up in her shawls and clothed in the rubble, she stooped over looking for them, her husband, Hector, and her son, Hector II. All she found was a fistful of earth which she carried in her apron pockets. All she found was a handful of sorrows before departing from the countryside in the solitude of the blood.

The Earthquake of Chillán

Carmen Carrasco told us that for days she drifted among the rubble of the infamous earthquake of Chillán of 1956, where the houses seemed like broken clay pitchers and where sadness howled like a one-armed demon. Carmen Carrasco told us that she looked for her son Hector Espindola among the ashes and incinerated rocks. She thought she had found his bare hands but then convinced herself that sometimes only the imagination rises from the dust of the rubble. This proved to be a consolation because she stopped grieving, thinking that Hector, like Lazarus, would bring her letters and singing birds so that she could hold them close to her heart.

Carmen Carrasco never stopped telling us about that

earthquake. She repeated that it was necessary to speak of the dead who suffer in order to perpetuate their life. This is why we believed in her powers and in her capacity to cure us from muscle spasms and asthma. Sometimes she would overwhelm us with kisses, would make us glimmer in love, and talk to us about happiness, about the magnificence of the air, of humidity and the sea. Only then would we fall asleep in the immensity of the prosperous night, but we would still hear her moan for her dead son and her hands would fill with dark dust and her forehead would cloister itself close to her sorrows.

Carmen Carrasco was eccentric and beautiful. They say that she went mad during the time of the earthquake in Chillán, but for us her's was a translucent soul. She walked with the rhythm of a seagull and of water and her calloused hands were like feasts of velvet for us. We did however notice the passing of her years in her harsh coughs and mature and desolate voice. Three days after the operation on her delicate gall bladder, she left for the south.

She left with a leg of roast pork, her sewing machine, and a rosary which, according to her, was from Jerusalem, but was actually from the occupied territory. They say that Carmencita died days later, happy with the pork in her pink, golden, and generous stomach. She died as she had lived, fearless and defiant.

Matilde Escobar

Matilde Escobar arrived at the house of my mother, recommended by her former English employers. At that time she was a very thin woman who madly loved truffles and who boasted about never having learned a word of English.

According to my mother, she was a magnificent keeper of keys. She used to maintain a very strict discipline with us children. We loved her but from a distance and with detachment, and it was impossible for us to cry nestled in her childlike breasts.

Matilde Escobar was forgetful and stubborn. She would spend hours arranging dying orchids as well as talking about the sins of sex and about the times when her desperate vagina called out in screams for someone to shave off the small cysts that sporadically appeared within her. Very few times she let my brother and me bathe together nude, so we couldn't delight in our very beautiful and bulging differences. Miss Escobar lived in the back rooms, in the darkness of the borrowed rooms for three years until my mother decided to fire her because of a damned alarm clock.

Matilde Escobar could not sleep because she lived pendent on the hours and minutes in which she would have to get up for the following day or for the masses she would attend in which a priest would give her the host which she would eat with a pleasure that resembled lust more than devotion. As a result, my generous mother then decided to buy her an alarm clock at the store of the Turk on the corner, a name we gave to all who came from the Middle East with semitic faces. When my mother gave her the gift, Miss Matilde grumbled and as usual confessed that she was always tired and worried about waking up and that those yawns which were as endless and obscure as the night itself accentuated her insomnia and were only signs of her responsible nature and not her stubborness.

She confessed her unfortunate need to live marking the rhythm of the seconds, and she talked about the times in which she couldn't wake up and dreamt about the end of the world and threatened herself for not waking up on time. Nevertheless, she detested the alarm clock and cautiously flung it at my mother's wavy head. It didn't decapitate her but was the cause of an irreparable rift between them.

I only remember seeing Matilde pack her faded and flowery robe and her tiny sandglass and stay awake the whole blessed night so as not to miss that train that would bring her to her next job as a servant, where she would continue to mark time by exhausting herself into a sickly fatigue because of her stubborn rejection of that magnificent electrical device that induces sleep.

Simply María

María arrrived at our house like so many other strange and displaced servants with worm-eaten shawls and a smell of grief. . . . She arrived starving and silent, like an odd and beloved witch. Her hair stuck to her body and head and something in her eyes irradiated either too much love or madness.

We began to love her and liked the warmth of her bedroom and the blankets of imitation wool from the southernmost region of the planet, that her godmother had given her when she reached her dreaded fifteenth birthday and went to the city, leaving behind the expansive countryside and perverse tranquility of familiar forests.

María liked radio soaps about love and restrained sex. During many years of my childhood I would settle comfortably very close to her, would rest immersed in her many fragrances, and would listen to a very long radio soap opera called *Esmeralda de los Ríos.* We cried together when Esmeralda was abandoned by her mother, a tale that somewhat resembled that of the Jews and the story of Moses but this time having nothing to do with the famous piece of yellow cloth in which Moses's mother wrapped him. Esmeralda de los Ríos was delivered like a fish, naked and lonely. Perhaps it was then that I managed to understand the special bond between Jews and servants. For instance, neither could enter a country club with the sole exception of a cousin of mine with a green pea face who passed for a French woman and adopted the name of her octogenarian husband, who, incidentally, had strong Indian features despite the fact that he denied his marvellous Pre-Columbian past.

With María I also learned that women ought to close their legs, shut their mouths, and shut the doors, but that it was all right for us to cry and sigh along with those beautiful, very rich, tear-jerking Mexican melodramas that had nothing to do with the austere and insular character of the Chilean people and of those from the contaminated Andean mountain range.

María suffered from too much love of life and drink. Sometimes on beach-going days when the heat was like a star-studded drowsiness, María would take us for a walk and drink something that looked like golden foam. She drank many bottles of this golden foam and we followed her bound for the shore. . . . She would stumble along in a very beautiful and fragile way and her blushed face would take on the color of the sunsets while her hands became two seagulls filled with that golden froth that she called her shield of gold.

In the summer María would go out at night. She suffered from spasms of insomnia and from stomach cramps. My parents looked at her with sadness and defiance and asked her please not to return to the stone house next to the sea at such unruly hours.

One strange night when the air grazed suspended on the motionless colors of the afternoon, and when holy families apparently gather together and think about peace, María arrived home wild and flaming mad, clutching a long carving knife that belonged to her lover, the butcher. Shouting out strange things in a silent and worm-eaten voice, she spoke to us of women, widows, duels, and of the rites of savage, cutting love.

This was my María, the one who scratched her hair and nose while she listened to Esmeralda de los Ríos and the one who said that Jews had horns in their scalp. This is my María who now wears the expression of the feared and naked things as she dances through the rooms. This is my María who seems to want to dream about death and to kill us with the knife of Don Juan, the butcher, the same Don Juan who sells us beef loin and ribs even though we know that here no one is kosher. This María holds us captive and wants to strip us of life. We look at her red hands and her black pupils peering out through her recently shaved hair like a shield of gold. Then my father asks her for her hand and she gives him the knife.

Etelvina Cuevas

Etelvina Cuevas was born in Río Colorado, a pre-Andean region. Since she was a young girl she walked barefoot through the snow-covered hills and thorny underbrush. She cared for sheep, old people, and deranged men and was born to look after human misery and sickness. She also was familiar with the timely faces of death and understood about absences and by-gone things.

She arrived at Valparaíso, driving back love affairs, and began to work at the home of my Aunt Luisa Smirnoff, the one who shut the eyes of the dead. There was something unusual about Etelvina; as soon as she arrived anywhere the wilted geraniums would bloom, the wheat flour would raise proudly, the obstructed pipes would unclog and whistle more than ever before, and the house would fill up with beautiful and strange individuals like my Grandmother Sonia from Odessa, who would teach her how to prepare cod Sebastopol style, and Señora Rebecca, who would arrive behind the illustrious Don Isaac to preach the rites of Judaism, as well as Francisco, the obsolete floor polisher, who died at the home of Aunt Luisa from excess, love, and wine. Everyone came to Luisa's house so that Etelvina could cure them with her mountain-like eyes and her watermelon heart.

Helena's mother, Frida, in Vienna, c. 1902.

Mauricio and Helena in Vienna, 1920.

Clara, Grandmother Helena's cousin, who perished in Auschwitz.

From left to right: Don Isaac, Joseph, my Grandmother Helena, Rebecca, and my mother Josephine, Osorno, 1939.

My Grandmother Helena's Polish passport. The last stamp in it is from Vienna, October 19, 1938.

THE VIENNESE LADY

My Grandmother Helena

My grandmother was Viennese and liked to write her name with an H. She was Frau Helena, the neighbor of Martin Buber in Vienna. She enjoyed reading Rilke and Goethe and she liked to go to the market to select fresh strawberries. In the afternoons she would meet in the cafes with her discreet and elegant girlfriends in order to talk about love and fleeting death.

In Santiago, Chile, amid the Andean winds, Frau Helena dreamt about the mountains of Austria, the wild-flowers, lilacs, and edelweiss. This way between sleep and wakefulness she would recreate her Viennese land-scapes, adamant and without ever forgetting that in those same forests they burned her Jewish girlfriends, that those same educated gendarmes came to her house looking for the necessary spoils of war, including her goose down pillows inherited on the day of her marriage to Isidoro Broder. Strangely those gendarmes loved music, burned Jews, and prohibited the killing of birds.

My grandmother was Viennese. In Santiago, Chile, she kept the secret of the war in her silky eyes while she walked with her gourds to the old coffee houses in the center of the city. Frau Helena would ask for strudel and would wait there for her friends who would arrive silent and remote with their tongues tied by cold and fear. They would then drink their coffee in silence, arching their arms with the faith of survivors, hiding tatoos. They consoled themselves talking about the rise in vegetable prices but all of them, in the remote distance, heard within their soul the sounds of the nebulous train, of the deranged train that would carry them to that ultimate destiny where the Viennese gendarmes would decide upon life or death by simply raising their little fingers.

My Grandmother Helena of the kaffe houses. Frau Helena, with her high-heeled shoes of a Viennese witch, returns on the road to the cordillera thinking about the Viennese woods and the padlocks of her house.

THE VIENNESE LADY

My Omama Helena

My Omama Helena and I had an alliance of women who carry baskets full of flowers and memories of exile, so when she reached that ambiguous, advanced territory of a childlike senility, I brushed her very fine locks as if they were lost threads in some silk bedspread or in some bride's trousseau. To me it seemed that in that long hair, which she only untied at midnight, and in the tranquility of her bedchamber, she had passed through the bonfires of demonized terror, had gotten involved in the holds of obscure boats, and on few occasions had been caressed by her handsome husband, my Grandfather Isidoro, "the chocolate soldier" dead in some meadow in the Vienna woods.

I learned many things from my Grandmother Helena; among these, how important walking is for our health and the two of us like strange lost souls with our high-heeled boots wandered through the cities of Osorno and Santiago always looking above toward the cordillera. I also learned to read Goethe and to speak German, even though I always had a strange misgiving for that language in which orders were given for all that was forbidden.

From my Grandmother Helena I learned that fragile silence is the silence of the wise. That silence that has nothing to do with the virtue of obedience in women is a precious gem. She would say that before getting angry one should maintain a profound silence and count to ten. I didn't ask her if she kept silent when they burned her house and the books of her neighbor, Martin Buber.

I learned to keep silent before ignorance, especially when they would shout at me and my brother in unison: "Who stole the bread from the ovens?" and the chorus would repeat, "The Jewish dogs." And, on our wedding day when my husband and I boarded the bus for our honeymoon and they said, "There go the Jewish dogs married to the devil."

My Grandmother Helena taught me to respect afternoon teas, to live a civilized life free from anxiety, to close my legs at the proper juncture, and never to raise my little finger when drinking tea in porcelain cups containing mandarin orange rinds.

I remember her every day, especially on silent nights here in this country, so far in the south as if it were a star at the end of the world. I also have hair filled with exiles and lost birds.

The Lady from Vienna

My Grandmother Helena, the fine lady from Vienna, would spend her winters in Santiago before an enormous window that faced the interior of my parents' home, a generous dwelling in a decent Santiago neighborhood that almost occupied half a block. In the middle of the garden was a palm tree brought from the island of Puerto Rico that grew with the velocity of love and relatives, tripling the pregnancies of my nearby and distant cousins. Omama Helena thought about her adored and distant Vienna with that silent snow shaped in a discreet silence.

Railroad Stations

At the end of the war, my Grandmother Helena, like an individual possessed and delirious, approached the railroad stations with a picture of her sisters on her severed chest. They were young and had faces that emanated goodness. They were kind souls burned in the sickly zones of gas. For years my Grandmother Helena tied her disjointed face and bleeding heart to the photographs of her dead sisters, and today I listen to their footsteps, those walks through the forests of wire.

My Grandmother Helena dreams about her sisters, creating mounds of grayish pillows, and she spends years thinking that they will disembark from the rail platform as they did before, in the days of love, before the war and the terror. She sees them there on the platform with their organdy blouses and their pure untarnished arms sprouting wings.

The Laced Gloves

My Grandmother Helena wore some very long ivory-colored lace gloves. Many times I felt the curiosity to actually see the color of her skin and approach the warm opening of her hands. However it remained concealed and hidden like her padlocks from Vienna, silent and thick. Years later I learned that my Grandmother Helena's arms were tatooed with the inexhaustible number of the concentration camp and this is why her arms remained concealed. Is there anything more unimagineable than branding people as if they were beasts? Why do they insist upon using the term *survivor* for those who escaped from the camps of hell? The survivors were people. They were victims like my Aunt Alma who was carried to the gas chambers, bareboned and tortured.

And those who were saved? Weren't people like my Grandmother Helena also victims? And her vanilla-colored gloves, were they not hiding the infamy of an unbelievable history?

The Jews

I remember the spirit of my grandmother as if it were a collage of legends connected with other histories. In my home they always talked as if we were people with a vast history, wandering protagonists in books about millenary lives that my grandfather called the disordered books of God.

My Grandmother Helena left her house in Vienna to her neighbor, Martin Buber. She left lentils and sweet basil soaking in the bathroom sink for good luck, and she said good-bye to the austere Austrian women who still were not afraid to greet her. She couldn't distribute the books in her library even though she knew that they would most likely end up in a diabolical pyre. She only took a huge eiderdown quilt with her and in Chile learned to divide it into three parts for her children.

My Grandmother Helena lost her jewels in deep ransacked trunks. She left wearing her silver-plated fox pins and her hat like the seas. She departed Vienna, its side streets and philosophy, and embarked on a freighter with thousands of other Jews who, like her, had abandoned their belongings and bodies but never lost their souls or their yearning gaze toward an open frontier.

Scenes of War

Scenes of war, gestures of all wars, left me speechless, and within me rose a city of silent towers and an expanding wave of terror and silences. I ask myself why is it that when the Jews gathered like obedient and quiet animals, no one shouted, no one said anything, no one approached them? Were we deserving of this dementia?

Why is it that when they hanged my Grandmother Helena's neighbor, not one person approached him even to shut his eyes?

Uncle Mauricio

When Mauricio abandoned Vienna, the coffee houses and those delirious love affairs beneath the strident music of a crackling cabaret, he cried for already lost objects but more than anything for his great friend, Hans, who followed him to the harbor in Hamburg from far away. There, together with his ashen-colored mother Helena, he approached the ship's deck.

The gestapo agent inspected all of the passers-by and those who embarked on the colorful small vessel with bleeding and toothless hearts.

With the laughter of the mediocre, Hans shouted to the guard that my uncle was wearing an embroidered jacket that was much too elegant for a Jew. The gendarmes, as a result, approached him very diligently and took the opportunity to undress him and humiliate his circumcised penis. When the whistles finally announced the departure for South America, Hans threw my uncle an old jacket containing a gold cigarette case hidden in one of the pockets. Mauricio disembarked on Chilean land with that magical and shiny object, he looked at the wild and rebellious hills of Valparaíso and with the gold cigarette case he amassed a fortune and recovered love's honor and the complete friendship of Hans: a proper and sincere German.

The Leica

Just like my Grandmother Helena who couldn't get rid of her feathers from Vienna, winged and delirious feathers like dreams of air and chloroform, my Uncle Mauricio also escaped Vienna bound for Hamburg with his most prized possession: a Leica camera. He hid it for three months on that undulating and sinister ship that carried thousands of Jewish passengers searching for a stable and healthy land in which to live. After arriving in Chile, however, he never worked as a photographer. He was a pastry cook, a hair dresser, and a singer in the Viennese choruses of the province, and he managed to sell the camera for not too paltry a sum. This is how he acquired enough money to create his first Chilean enterprise involving silver articles. My Uncle Mauricio had a good eye. He chose his friendships and surnames wisely and married a young woman from the Chilean aristocracy. However, we poor and uncultured Jewish relatives were not invited to their presumptuous, mediocre, and perverse parties. They didn't like to hear me pray in Hebrew because that ancient and noble melody was foreign to the hearts of those arrogant Christians. When my uncle died, we never saw each other again, and for my seventeenth birthday my aristocratic aunt gave me a jar of conserved peaches.

Hope Chests

They always ask me if my Grandmother Helena had managed to salvage certain objects from her home in Vienna, but she never spoke to me of lost objects or about that night of the maimed crystal when they started to slash the eiderdown quilts and silk shawls with crimson-colored knives and fill the rooms with fear and smoke. I only remember the delicate and tall silver candlesticks in Osorno with which Frau Helena would make her altars of light very late in the afternoon, when the Chilean sky opens like a generous and never foreign hand.

My Grandmother Helena slowly lit the candlesticks

from Vienna and prayed for the enemy, for the warriors deranged by war, and for all those who didn't have time to pray or to repent. She prayed for peace for the Indians, for her dead sisters, and for the children on the last trains of terror.

I now keep the Viennese candlesticks in my home, and although I don't pray, I talk to God and get angry with Him and ask him about those who have no homeland.

My Grandmother Helena possessed the nobility of the enlightened and the silent. She was a grande dame of few words and believed in the subtleties of a facial expression. She advised me to take seven sips of water before speaking and from her I learned to respect the cadences of silence. They say that the young women of the Austrian countryside wished to work for her in Vienna because upon entering her home she would buy them an enormous hope chest, which she would little by little fill with goose-down quilts, blue tablecloths, and little gems and camisoles of tulle for their future wedding day.

When the Germans ransacked her home, the young girls happily had managed to rescue the love trunks, and the desperate gendarmes found only clippings from diaries and two darkened padlocks from an imaginary house in the country.

Star of David

My grandmother gave us a Star of David. It was small and tarnished and had the color of a time-worn lady. Sometimes, when my brother and I looked at it with a combined expression of tenderness and dream, it seemed like a genuine phosphorescent star that watched over the health of the sick and accompanied the dead to their final resting places. My grandmother told us that it was an honor always to wear it close to the chest, the same way old ladies wore their sweaty cameos tied to their pudgy necks. For me that star was like the threshold of certain forbidden territories that led to the nebulous chasms of war, of that war where they burned trees and Jewish girls, of that very strange war that carried my aunts on the trains of the evil omens. But when we took our walks in the afternoons filled with a reddish and always passing light, we liked to show our star, we liked the people of the town to know that we too could hang pretty things around our necks, even if they were not dark and somber-looking crosses.

We had a star that swayed back and forth, had six points and, more than anything, was our very own. However, sometimes I heard them say: "There go the Marranos, the Jews, the Hebrews," and only the little Indian girls, the "cholitas" as they were called in the town, approached without spitting at us. They approached us in order to touch the Star of David, to rub it and get it to glitter as if it were a thread on a magical gown. And they, the "cholitas," didn't spit at us and didn't cross over to the other side of the street when we passed by.

The Eiderdown Comforter

When they talked about superstitions in my family, my father's voice would get raspy and he would say that "those are matters having to do with goys; we don't believe in false superstitions." However, on the nights and days of death, when we covered the mirrors with torn sheets and when angels of death and life were talked about, I was happy and more like the others because my religion which was so austere and silent finally made it possible for me to believe in the magic of imagery.

I also don't believe in superstition or reincarnation, but now that I am older and a little less wise, I see myself as the reincarnation of my Grandmother Helena, the noble woman from Vienna. I remember or am made to recall that when the Nazis knocked at her crystal door, she hid her beloved feathered pillows and comforters. They were part of her dowry; they were the memory and the breath of her nights of love.

From Hamburg to Valparaíso, those winged feathers like guardian angels were the means of my grandmother's repose when she traveled outdoors with fearless nature and the terrifying nostalgia of exiles.

I also recovered the fine feathered pillows and quilts. Yesterday when the weather seemed mild and the star-streaked sunlight covered the atmosphere, I began to create little dreams of love and not war. The furious wind, like the gendarmes in all countries, then tried to steal my feathers. Dispossessed I ran behind them, entangled and choking, and the roguish and dark wind robbed me of my precious possessions. I then invoked the name of my Grandmother Helena and the wind changed into an enormous blanket of sun, the feathers returned to my hands and I fulfilled my pledge. I followed those disenchanted generations of the future.

THE VIENNESE LADY

Candlesticks
My Grandmother
Helena
the lady from Vienna
the wandering dancer
only brought
from her city
the silver
candlesticks
the family tablecloth
and the pallor
of the padlocks
buried
within her bleeding
skirts.

The Vienna Woods

In the Vienna woods a Jewish girl plays amid the thickets and the brightness. In the Vienna woods very close to the soul of Franz Kafka, a Jewish girl sinks her lips into the harsh contours of the verdant soil. All of the woods in Vienna enclose the city as if they were a solitary crimson wire, as if the trees and history were also deeply rooted for the sole purpose of tying up the Jewish girl who still believes in the earth and the clearing of the woods.

In the Vienna woods, at a distance, a pack of hot-tempered men call the Jewish girl. They don't let her have the mist, the space, or the trees that are foreign to fascism.

In the Vienna woods, a Jewish girl relinquishes her hair amid the bonfires.

Star of Stanislav

Among the many tales I heard, my favorites were the stories of my aunts who came from what was then known as Stanislav, a village of the Austro-Hungarian Empire. However, now that its borders have dissolved or, better said, have been transformed into the thresholds of other nations, Stanislav is today a part of the former Soviet Union and very little is known about the Jews who lived there, among them my aunts who, according to my father, were both beautiful and serene. They loved to fill themselves with gazes and words. One of them had the soul and face of a bird. She attended all the meetings and this is why they brought her to Auschwitz. She thought that it would only be for a few days, that her anxiety would pass and that soon she would return to the flow of time and pass through the leaf-filled forests. But she only passed through the forests of wire. They shaved off her hair, but all the same, her eyes remained clear and serene. She had an expression of life and hope frozen on her dead mouth.

When I think of Stanislav, I think about my Aunt Estella. I imagine her with her eyes half-opened looking like the gestures of flowing rivers. I imagine her ready and surrendering to the blue sargasso of the gas chambers.

Talking About War

When they talked at home about the war and the "camps" that had nothing to do with sprawling poppy fields, we knew that they were referring to the spiked stretches of barbed wire, even though my Grandmother Helena used to say that sometimes in the camps they would let her see that brilliant strip of poppies that grew inflamed between the rocks and wire. For Helena all that remained from Germany was its language, that same language that obliged her to strip and to tie up her hair so as later to have it shaved off, that same language that forbade her to go to the movies and to school, to touch the trees and go out into the street.

This is why I like Spanish. It tastes like something sweet and remote, and although it has a relationship with the word for inquisition, it is a language for love and not for prohibiting or giving orders or incinerating the hair of my Grandmother Helena.

Helena's Dolls

Among all the beloved objects and those which bring me closest to happiness are those which populate and respond to my memories of Omama Helena. Her Viennese friends from Santiago called her Frau Helena. My Grandmother Helena loved books and kept them underneath her bed, especially those with shabby travel-worn covers that had crossed the seas and exiles. She kissed and underlined them and also kept between their pages pieces of her silky, delicate off-white hair that were like the color of full moons and the souls of lonely women.

Thanks to my Grandmother Helena, I learned German as a young girl. I also learned to read the German poets and philosophers. Reading was very important to her. Together with poetry, she believed that books should be read aloud. For my grandmother books were like homes where Jews could live united as in the kingdom of dream. Gazing at the lips of Helena, I learned the word *utopia,* that sense of not being in any particular place, and I felt confused by the transparent revelation of the word.

For years, my Grandmother Helena played with dolls, the same dolls that we used to hide in the coffins. She taught us to dress them and to close their legs and hands because the rules of feminine etiquette were important to her. Through time, my grandmother herself became a round, old, and beautiful doll who lost her memory and forgot about the sounds of war, about the candlesticks and the severed smoke of her dead sisters. She talked as if she were praying while my brother and I caressed her, swaying back and forth with her straight and transparent ash-colored hair. She was our big doll roaming about and lighting her antique candlesticks that now live in my home.

We never knew if Helena had elected childhood as another way of inventing her sliced life. She would cut up little pieces of colored paper, which she would incrust within the travel-worn covers of her sacred books. She also would steal little coins from her son's coat. Aware of this, he would leave her some small change upon returning from work and she would go back to her childhood on the streets of Vienna and to her plumed hats when no one called her a wretched Jew, when she played with colorful pieces of paper and they didn't tell her that Jewish girls were the daughters of the devil and of swine.

Omens

Death visiting us like a sortilege and omen. It announces itself behind the coolness of the air and beneath the texture of the stormy weather. We feel it appearing in the cracks. Carmencita looks for her shawls. My Viennese grandmother says that she doesn't believe in the legends of these Indians. She then takes out her silk-covered Bible and asks the servants to cover the mirrors as her grandparents had done. The Indian women cross themselves and cover the irascible mirrors. The house in the South prepares itself for death that announces itself in the roar of a few scrawny horses. Death without its carriages and hats of mist only arrives at the thresholds but it cannot see itself in the mirrors.

Landscapes

After the exile and silent censorship and after the voyage from very deep within myself, tatooed in memories,

I return to my home where the araucarias taught me that I am a temporary fragment of history within the larger histories of life. I return and there is the house with its straw roof, red floor tiles, and salamanders that smell of remote times and spaces. In the distance of the dawn, I then approach the drawing room of the house where my father, Joseph, listens to the stories of walled-up Germany and where my mother sits at the table, silent and foreign. Frau Helena appears praying for the Indians and for the Jews but especially for all of our dead cousins. I return home and I see them. They also see me. They wait for me and we kiss. Then I know that my journey has ended and that this sonata was an omen from God.

A young girl named Frida looks at herself in the mirrors. She approaches the dining rooms and finds her dead grandmothers with a victrola that sings Russian songs and curls up in the absences like the furniture.

Lilacs

Between the distances and beyond the southern vapors, my father brought me through the streets of his Vienna, through imaginary walks so as to portray that furrowed countenance of a city veiled behind the landscapes of perfidious and lucid histories. Beyond dreams, I gazed toward a network of crossings, of parks with landscapes of love and I learned about those streets where the evening dancers would doze with their heavy and tingly furs covering long encounters with nebulous lovers.

I loved the smell of lilacs with profound devotion, that sleepy and dense fragrance that would inundate me with an aching happiness in nights of illusion and haste. The lilacs of Pratter were not foreign to me; I recognized them as if I were a native inhabitant of that place, never mistaken by the distances imposed by the history of that harmful geography.

I also learned about when Vienna, the city of the lilacs, stopped emitting subtle hollyhock fragrances and only the footsteps of the gendarmes and the cunning jibes shifting about the avenues could be perceived, turning sacred locations into captive and worn-out memories.

In adulthood, sometimes one returns to certain cities, sure of having never left them behind. I returned to that Vienna inhabited in the thresholds of dream and idle childhood. I returned to search for the grave of my grandfather, Isidoro, my father's father. I didn't find lilacs on his grave or mirrors showing me the way. His grave lay lean and in solitude among the weeds, covered with dirt and the vestiges of broken human life in that abandoned Jewish cemetery in the center of the city.

THE VIENNESE LADY

I knelt down on the earth and covered his tombstone with my open hands that had made innumerable voyages before arriving there, and while cleaning it, I traveled through all of Vienna, the dark and diurnal city, the forests and all of the caresses of the good and sacred night. The inscription read: "Here lies a good man." Today those are the same words that accompany the grave of my father, Joseph, in Santiago, Chile, so far away from Pratter. I always leave him a bunch of lilacs, a current of green air, and cherries from this new continent.

Frida on her wedding day, Santiago,
June 19, 1948.

Frida Halpern and Moisés Agosín on their wedding day.

Josephine and Joseph at Frida's wedding, Santiago,
June 19, 1948.

Frida and her father Joseph, June 19, 1948.

Moises dressed as a Russian soldier, Chile, c. 1927.

From left to right: Grandmother Sonia, Frida, Josephine;
in front: Frida's daughters, Marjorie and Cynthia,
in Viña del Mar, March 1959.

Grandmother Sonia in Viña del Mar, 1970.

MY HUSBAND

Moses Saved from the Waters

He was a rather short and bald medical student. Sometimes I would see him carry gigantic skeletons through the parks. At other times he carried the skulls of extinct animals or of distinguished, crestfallen gentlemen. He would sit on wet wooden benches in the most ephemeral squares and would talk with his friends the bones. I also supposed that they too had already entered the beginning stages of eternity and of baldness. This is how I met my husband, in the Plaza de Armas close to our house. He studied in the afternoons on the same bench and would talk with the same skull and give a few coins to the forever toothless gypsies. I knew then that he was an ordinary and eccentric being with an enormous bow tie and that in the middle of winter, he wore shorts that revealed skinny and hairless legs.

I didn't know whether to feel a strange mixture of repulsion, curiosity, or tenderness for him. However, his presence drew me each time closer to the rhythm of life.

Moses was also my mother's first cousin and for this reason he lived in my home, which had been converted into a boardinghouse for poor relatives who came to study in the capital. I watched him for two years and he told me that he loved my violet-colored eyes and my firefly voice. I didn't ask him to swear eternal love but I did ask him to do my biology assignments, to dissect flies and frogs, and in moments of delirium I also asked him to translate some fragments of Shakespeare for me or to invent a lover's quarrel.

Friends

My friends envied me, but I doubt if they would have wanted to kiss the shiny bald head of Moses. I always felt him close to me and sometimes on foolhardy late afternoons I would watch him play Chopin's *Nocturnes* until very late at night. One time my mother flung two sharp-pointed shoes at his head and my father, his gold dentures, because Chopin's rhythms were intolerable at such an unfortunate hour of the day.

That same night he announced his departure to us

and said: "Tomorrow I will leave and take my piano but later I will come for your daughter."

And so it was that years later I saw my future husband again because my Grandmother Helena was gravely ill and needed enormous transfusions of blood. By gathering together his robust medical companions, Moses managed to save the tired veins of my Viennese lady. I remember that among the strongest men was an Arab who donated abundant supplies of blood, which set off an alarm of panic in my home over the mere thought that my Grandmother Helena would be cured with enemy blood. But this is how it was, and thanks to this generous Arab Helena lived to be ninety-two years old and continued traveling on foot through the streets of Santiago and meeting with her dear friends to talk about the war and about the Viennese woods.

Years later I married the eccentric doctor and was happy. We had children and I also learned to talk with his skulls that emitted a strange warmth resembling the breath of living beings.

Trains

We met on a railway platform on a transfer train in Valparaíso, at the edge of the water, with our faces outlined on the glass. He talked to me about my eyes and their capacity for holding wonder. I looked at him perplexed and knew from that moment that I would marry him. Years later I discovered that we were distant cousins although we never played together in dark rooms.

The Possibilities of Ire

The possibilities of ire and hatred accumulated in those days of the war in that very small and distant country surrounded by vast and imaginary blizzards and pools of water, that country where the people dressed in dark tones because of their taciturn nature and that country that sheltered my father and my grandmother from the spoils of Nazi war and was also an advocate of Hitler's Germany until almost the end.

During the effervescence of the war, Chile was seized by a German frenzy. The number of German schools and parades through the squares tripled, and strange dark individuals who had nothing to do with the Aryan desire wore tied to their arms the insolent and for them invigorating swastika.

The man who is now my husband was shouted at for being a Jew, for being a young man, and for being brilliant. Mediocrity is also part of the legacy of hatred. However, he knew how to defend himself because of his surgeon's training. . . . He carried small bundles of knives in his unadorned pockets. At that time he was persecuted so much that they even prevented him from buying a cadaver for his anatomy lessons. Nevertheless, Moses, an able survivor familiar with the persecution of his father in Crimea, knew that it would be in his best interests to become friends with the gravedigger, who supplied him with a beautiful cadaver named Luchito from the public cemetery. He would hang Luchito inside the closet of his narrow room at the boarding house. Luchito was his best friend in the days of the war in which the souls of Chileans were agitated and disturbed while they loved listening to clandestine German radio broadcasts and they talked with joy about the experiments of Mengele who also left behind his devastating tracks in the zones of southern Chile. Years later in 1973, the military junta recovered the German horror, the obscure Nazi tactics of making people disappear. My country filled up with a sinister lexicon . . . these were the fateful days of the war, with the infernal mist of the *nacht und neblen*.

Alejandro 1947

My mother hated all of my suitors and admirers, as she used to call them. She hated the cadets with their blue capes and thin sabers, she hated Alejandro with his dentist's brief case, but more than anything she hated the one who was going to become my husband: bald-headed Moses, as they called him because he was born with little hair. Moses was one of those privileged beings. He was born bald. He liked to hang up X-ray pictures of his dead patients and he kept the skull of his first patient as a mascot.

My dear Moses loved all these immense and amorphous structures of bones and memories. He didn't use them to decorate his room at the boardinghouse, but rather kept them for good luck, since he didn't like the thought of separating himself from that cranium that accompanied him during his truculent first year as a medical student.

Moses also had a piano that seemed to fly with the melodies of Mozart, Chopin, and Beethoven at three o'clock in the morning. My parents could no longer tolerate waking up unhinged by Beethoven's funeral march and they kicked him out of the house. He merely responded with, "Tomorrow I will come to look for the piano and next month for your daughter." At any rate we got married and Adolfito's skull was given to my Uncle Gollo who put it next to his night stand and hid it from the sight of beautiful women who opened their mouths in awe whenever he told them about his triumphs as a dental surgeon.

Foreigners

It was during the time of the war or a few years before that we discovered that in Chile they also didn't want the Jews. The animosity, the hatred, presented themselves in strange forms, in certain tones of the voice, as for example in phrases like "You, foreigners" or things like: "You always have your country, Israel." "We" and "you," two amorphous words, created strange cities and distant harbors in daily speech. My Grandmother Helena kept silent and devoted herself to cutting clippings from newspapers, colored ribbons and gift wrap so as to pacify her nerves, so as not to think about her incinerated first cousins, with their hair floating amid the mist of smoke.

At that time, Moses and I were engaged. He defended himself against antisemitic attacks with a special knife that he utilized to open skulls. It was a savage knife which he hid in the pocket of his medical uniform. That sacred and secret knife never terrified me. Far to the contrary, it protected me from fear and made me feel privileged by its side. Sometimes I liked to touch it, and I felt happy being able still to become fond of that threatening object.

I remember that on Sundays Moses and I liked going to the shore, and on rare occasions when my father allowed me, we went to Valparaíso to visit my uncles and aunts and also walk through the disheveled and irascible streets of the city. One day we went to the dock because some mysterious whales, very fat and panting for life, had arrived at the harbor, beautiful in every repugnant sense of their dripping blubber.

Moses and I climbed on board a rowboat called the *Tom Thumb* because it was small and seemed like something out of a tale about hungry children. The oarsman was semicross-eyed and had a wooden leg which produced in me a mixed sensation of fear and pleasure. It was in that boat resembling paper that Moses asked me to marry him, but I had to promise him that I would never go out with another cadet or even look at one in the eyes. Confused, I said yes. I swore to him that I loved him, knowing with certainty that no cadet would ever wrap me in his profoundly deep cape and that I would never walk with him on bright, moonlit nights or beneath the Andean wind. At that time I saw myself as the eternal companion of that doctor who made me happy. I loved his baldness and his silence.

The Doctors

When my husband, Moses, had just received his medical degree during the sinister war years, wise doctors arrived escaping the Hitlerian dementia in order to re-make their lives in Chile and to practice acts of good faith which represent medicine's most noble task. Some antisemitic doctors would humiliate Moses, ask him cruel questions, and make him talk about the blue gas chambers, so as ultimately to deny him the right to practice medicine.

However, when my husband obtained a more powerful position and was an examiner for the Jewish doctors who arrived in Chile daily, he used to talk with them for many hours and tell them about Mozart and his parents in Odessa. They, nervous and confused, would ask him, "Doctor, when will you give us the exam?" and bald-headed Moses would say "Don't worry, you know more about medicine than I do. The exam is over."

Santiago 1948

I got married on June 19, 1948, the year Israel stopped being called Palestine and became a free, independent state. All ideas regarding Zionism were for us remote matters; we only believed that finally we would have something to call a nation and that our identity would be rooted to the earth. Despite having three generations born in Chile, good-natured and unscrupulous friends always ask us if we will return someday to our country, Israel, forgetting that I too was born in Chile as well as my brother and our children and the children of our children.

On my wedding day the lilacs that my father loved so much because they reminded him of the Viennese woods before the day of hatred and dung, blossomed. Carmencita, that faithful woman who I never considered a servant but rather as a victim of earthquakes and misfortune, combed my very long hair that I cut only after three years of marriage since my husband the doctor was incapable of charging his patients, and money was extremely scarce.

My Grandmother Helena had left the stove lit the night before and through a strange twist of fate the second floor of the house began to burn. All I did was beg the firefighters to salvage my wedding gown and the goose-down quilt that she had given to me. Happily my winged wedding gown resembling angels more than Jewish brides was rescued from the flames, and when I began to establish my household, my husband and I caressed each other beneath those Viennese feathers. Our breathing confused itself with the rhythms and dreams of love. We were happy. Our children were eventually born and on their wedding day, they also snuggled in those goose-down comforters, closer to desire than to nights of war.

A Luxuriant Heart

We liked the fall and the yellow hearts of the leaves. Some of that splendor remained in our bodies, something from those things that illuminate within the barefoot body that crosses the thickness of the moss.

You and I between the leaves, tossing and turning in the immensity of the air that grazes us, making us each time more ourselves and less sensible and uncovered. Fall in the distance is a mermaid with algae and amber stones on her breasts. You tread on my body as if you were a feast, a tablecloth of leaves ready for sleep, ready to feel your fishlike walk in my hands, in my eyes that palpitate like a yellow heart.

Fall brings us closer to the clarity of the body that kindles in the luminous air. I sail on your footsteps, you release me from the silky vestments, and we thus remain motionless like the roots of the leaves, like the luxuriant and mercilessly bare forests.

Soliloquy

To name love like a soliloquy or a gesture filled with
surprises and luminous canvasses.
Love like a silence that approaches to warm us up and
whisper
in our ear.

Of all languages, I prefer that of love like the
sound of flowing water and reddish dresses worn in the
wild freshness of carnival days.

To name love is to approach,
to have your body at my side
to feel the warmth without saying it, approaching my
ear, to imagine fragrances.

To write love in the vestibules of the night,
in the dining rooms
where bloody, volatile
gifts are offerred, to write love as if you were a
firefly when you approach me to anoint
my ankles.

My Husband

I

Night engulfing
capturing in its
ailing womb
all the obscurity
that proliferates and sings,
all the severed
obscurity
that enters as in an
incandescent vapor.

II

Night tinted
with evil omens
gathering us up with its sharp
words
and chloroform dreams

III

Night engulfing us more each time,
stretching us like a
perverted witch
night, the night like
a sick
crack
like a molded obscurity
of scars
night, absences.

IV

The night
like Lazarus resurrecting
with air
life
dance.

EPILOGUE

I emerge from the unmasked shadow and suddenly, my house smells like the lilacs of Pratter and the wild lilacs that bloom in the forests of my Chile. The fragrance covers me as if it were filled with omens of peace. The lilacs remind me of my dead aunts, my father's loves, and the afternoons when we covered the mirrors, while in the barbed-wire camps of Europe the bodies of thousands upon thousands of *figuren* covered the cumbersome and twisted earth.

My father used to say that it was very difficult being a Jew. I still think there is a lot of truth in his words, but more than anything there is a lot of beauty and good fortune. We survived, we took refuge in the last corner of the planet in that stretch of land lost between blizzards and tides. We survived exiles, foreign tongues, and jibes from the daily inferno. We always were the "others," those foreigners who believed in the Sabbath and prayed to an irate and invisible God. We were a people of solitude with a memory like tatoos.

Throughout all these years and with all my insomnias, I am a happy and grateful woman; I possess no animosities or remorse. My memory is also an immense meadow of bellflowers and trains of refugees that approach and become transfigured by the pulse, the breath of a new life with songs of peace.

I return to the blue kitchen of Osorno, to the kisses beneath the eiderdown quilts and my memory approaches the generous hands of Carmencita dressing me and brushing my braids of a Jewish princess. My hands were never surrounded by barbed wire. My hands only touched the prophecies of love.

I approach the South and the last frontier of my country. It is a beautiful country that seems as if it were a perpetual forest of vapors and fragrances; a star too distant to reach faith. My Grandmother Helena taught me how to dry roses, to name trees, to light candles, to remember the dead, and to predict the migratory routes of the birds; my nanny Carmencha, to celebrate St. John's Eve and to recite the Our Father. I learned so much in those solitudes, but more than anything I remember my father waiting at the train stations with his summerlike eyes and his hands filled with lilac and copihue blossoms as if old Vienna and new Chile co-existed in the generous, bursting foliage of his hands.